Grandparents, grandchildren
and the generation in between

D R G AY O CHILTREE

ACER Press

First published 2006
by ACER Press
Australian Council *for* Educational Research Ltd
19 Prospect Hill Road, Camberwell, Victoria, 3124

Edited by Kerry Biram
Cover and text design by Divine Design
Typeset by Baseline Design
Printed by Hyde Park Press

National Library of Australia Cataloguing-in-Publication data:

Ochiltree, Gay.
   Grandparents, grandchildren and the generation in between.

   ISBN 978 0 86431 413 0.

   ISBN 0 86431 413 2.

   1. Grandparents - Australia. 2. Grandparenting - Australia.
   3. Grandparent and child - Australia. 4. Grandparents as
   parents - Australia. I. Title.

306.8745

Visit our website: www.acerpress.com.au

Foreword

Rituals and transitions are an important part of every society and every culture. They form an important part of the historical fabric, ground participants in something bigger than themselves, and ensure continuity from one generation to the next. Some rituals and transitions are present in all cultures—marriage, the birth of a child—and have been recognised forever. They are deeply rooted in sociological context and historical events.

In modern times in Western societies we have seen the introduction of newer rituals, such as the celebration of Mothers' Day, and more recently the marking of particular dates to focus one's attention on certain groups in the community (families, women, secretaries) or specific areas such as National Literacy and Numeracy Week.

Grandparents have no special day named after them, no ritual or rite of passage, no way of celebrating the extraordinary contribution they make. In the opening sentence of this book, Gay Ochiltree writes 'Grandparents are everywhere, yet they are often taken for granted'. Not only are they seemingly ignored by the popular media, but until very recently they have also been largely ignored by researchers. Compared to the voluminous body of research about parents and parenting, there is still an extraordinarily small amount of research about grandparents and grandparenting. Similarly, little consideration has been given to grandparenting as an important phase of adult development.

Grandparents play many roles in our society. They provide child care, in some cases episodic but often on a regular basis; sometimes because of family circumstances grandparents take primary responsibility for raising children. They provide advice (not always appreciated) to the child's parents, offer moral and sometimes financial support, and as Ochiltree writes '... grandparents are the glue that holds many families together when the going gets rough and there is nowhere else to turn'.

For most grandparents, their grandchildren are a source of great joy and pleasure in their lives. Grandparenting gives them an opportunity to reconnect with the magic world of young children. However, it can also be a source of considerable stress. Some grandparents resent expectations put on them about involvement with young children, especially when many still have their own busy lives or career to focus on. For others, this added responsibility comes at a time when they are relishing the new-found freedom that comes with the phase of life when their own children have become independent. Often there is conflict around child rearing styles or when there is a difficult relationship with their child's partner, and there may be the additional stress that comes from parents separating or blended families. Grandparenting is thus not always a positive experience, and certainly not all of the time.

In this important new book, Dr Gay Ochiltree writes about many aspects of grandparenting. A respected and experienced researcher herself, Dr Ochiltree has drawn widely on the existing research to write a compelling and absorbing book about grandparents and grandchildren. A considerable portion of Dr Ochiltree's career has focused on studying and then writing about families and children. She uses her very extensive academic experience to frame the research so that it illustrates many of the issues about grandparents and grandparenting that have hitherto been largely neglected. She shares from her own personal experience of being a grandparent, and quotes freely from interviews that she has conducted with grandparents across a diverse range of backgrounds and circumstances.

Although it is not designed to be a 'how to' book, it does represent a wonderful seamless mix of interpretation of research, personal opinion and observation, and accounts of the experience of others. In this regard, I am sure that this book will end up being a very useful resource for all grandparents, and may also help parents to understand some of the issues that many grandparents grapple with in what is normally a very joyous phase of their lives.

Dr Ochiltree's fluid and accessible writing style means that this book can easily be read from cover to cover. On the other hand, there are chapter headings and sections that can be used almost as a textbook, providing useful information and resources. These include, for example, grandparents and career; grandparenting styles and family involvement; grandparents and personal development; grandparents' relationship with their own children; grandparents' own health and wellbeing; grandchildren following divorce and remarriage; and diversity in grandparenting. The final chapter—'Child development and parenting'—is particularly useful as a guide for grandparents. This chapter covers the normal development of children at varying ages, together with strategies for the management of the sorts of challenging behaviours that are likely to occur at each age.

Grandparents, grandchildren and the generation in between is a wonderfully compre-hensive book from an accomplished author which celebrates grandparents: the joys and stresses, the ups and downs. Addressing a hitherto largely neglected phase of adult development, it is an important contribution and will be a valuable resource not only for grandparents but for all those interested in young children.

Professor Frank Oberklaid
Director, Centre for Community Child Health
Royal Children's Hospital, Melbourne
University of Melbourne

Contents

Dedicated to my grandmother Grace Henderson who died when
I was five but whose warmth and affection lives on.

Many grandparents gave up their time to be interviewed for this book and shared their experiences, both the happy and satisfying and the disappointing; for this I am very grateful. Some interviews were very sad but I felt great admiration for what these grandparents were doing and for the way that they had often put aside their own lives in the interests of their grandchildren.

Chapter 1

The contemporary grandparent

Grandparents are everywhere, yet they are often taken for granted. Grandparents go to playgrounds with their grandchildren, they pick them up after school, they take them to see the Wiggles or the latest children's film, they care for them when their parents are working and some grandparents are even bringing up their grandchildren. Grandparents are contributing to society more than they ever have before. Most are making enormous investments in the coming generation and supporting their children's generation in numerous ways. Most grandparents invest time, money, love, attention and care in their grandchildren. Nevertheless, it is not always easy being a grandparent.

We do not know how many grandparents there are in Australia, and what proportion of the population they represent, but increased longevity means that there are more grandparents today than there were in the past. Parents who become grandparents in their fifties may spend more than two decades of their lives as grandparents. Parents who become grandparents at a younger age may be grandparents for half their lives, and some may go on to become great-grandparents. Grandparents in the Indigenous community are the exception to this, although they are likely to become grandparents at a young age. However they are unlikely to spend so much of their lives as grandparents because of a shorter life expectancy due to disadvantage and poor living conditions which are associated with the loss of land, of culture and of language, and the forcible removal of many children from their families.

More than a quarter of a million babies are born in Australia each year and most have between one and four grandparents. Some of these grandparents already have grandchildren but for others it is the first grandchild and usually greeted with special pleasure. As the numbers of grandparents increase, and the baby boomers born in the 20-odd years following World War II become grandparents, there is a growing awareness of the role grandparents play in the community.

In Western societies such as Australia, grandparents are on the whole better educated, healthier, and live longer than they did in the past. Grandparents are usually still in the workforce when their first grandchild is born, yet images of grandparents often do not reflect these changes. The image of the little white-haired grandmother in her rocking chair doing her knitting and the little old grandfather tottering around the garden is not in keeping with 21st-century reality. Grandmothers have changed more than grandfathers because of the increasing number of women in paid employment; far fewer women these days remain at home until they are older and retired. On the other hand, with people living longer, the image of aged grandparents is not altogether inaccurate because, although grandparents are usually fit and relatively young when they first become grandparents, they age in the role as their grandchildren grow and develop, and as other grandchildren and sometimes great-grandchildren are born.

Whether they are in paid employment or not, grandparents are usually involved with their grandchildren to some extent. Most grandparents spend time with their grandchildren, many babysit and some provide child care. While it is grandmothers who are usually more involved, grandfathers are also active in their grandchildren's lives. A visit to any child care centre or school shows the extent to which grandparents are involved in dropping off grandchildren in the morning and picking them up in the afternoon. Many preschools and primary schools invite grandparents to visit on special days so that they can meet the teachers and child care staff and see what their grandchildren are doing. Grandparents can also regularly be seen in parks and playgrounds with their grandchildren, and even quite elderly grandparents play some role. Many migrant parents—but mostly grandmothers—are almost fully occupied in the care of grandchildren until they go to school.

Grandparents are relatively taken for granted in most Western society although they have recently been getting more recognition. There is no rite of passage, no special reward, and no special day to celebrate grandparents in the way that Mother's Day and Father's Day is celebrated. While many may regret the materialism of the current Mother's Day and Father's Day 'retail opportunities', these designated days do draw the attention of the broader community to the importance of mothers and fathers. However, I recently read about a Grandparents' Day on a Sunday in early September in the United States, but it does not appear to be widespread. If the idea catches on it is likely to eventually be imported here like so much other American culture, and may make some positive impact.

In some cultures grandparents have an important and esteemed role in society. They are also more likely to be respected for their age, especially in those Asian societies based on Confucian values where filial piety is important. In some South-East Asian communities grandmothers have an important traditional role after the birth of a baby. The mother is confined for around a month after the birth to rest and regain her health and strength, and during this time she and the baby are cared for by female family members including the paternal grandmother. However, the status of grandparents may be changing in Western societies, as it is in Australia, where parents of young children are increasingly relying on the help of grandparents to care for their children. Nevertheless, reliance on the assistance and support of grandparents does not always guarantee respect.

The role of a grandparent is a dynamic one which changes as their family changes, as family members marry, divorce, and move away, and as children grow up and grandparents grow old. As children develop and their worlds expand and are influenced by modern technology and the Internet, the worlds of many grandparents are contracting as they grow older, retire and leave the workforce and lose touch with the advances in technology that are part of the everyday lives of their grandchildren. As grandparents grow older their incomes are usually also reduced and some will have reduced physical capacities as their health declines with age. These factors influence what they can do with their grandchildren. On the other hand, grandparents are now likely to have more time to spend with their grandchildren. Migrant grandparents may also find that with the changes associated with the modern world, their traditional values come under challenge from the younger generations of their family. Nevertheless, children often find that their grandparents present other views of their family history and can provide them with other perspectives on their parents as their grandparents tell stories about them when they were children.

While grandfathers play an important role in the family, and sometimes try to make up for not spending enough time with their own children, in most cases it is the grandmothers who play a more significant role. They have a greater stake in family relations and are sometimes known as the 'kin keepers'. Women not only provide support in times of trouble but play a significant role in keeping family members in touch and informed. This is not to say that men do not have a role to play but they are more likely to be instrumental and practical in their approach. Alice Rossi, in her book *The Changing Contract Across the Generations*, which discusses relationships between the generations, concludes:

> The triad of grandmother, daughter, and grandchildren, supplemented by female siblings and their children, provides not only open hearts, but open doors and open purses in times of need and trouble. These women represent not only latent resources in bad times, but ongoing social support in good times as well (Rossi 1993, p. 209).

Women take on much of the responsibility for intergenerational continuity within the family. Intergenerational research has found that generally there are closer bonds between paternal grandfathers and grandsons and maternal grandmothers and grand-daughters. Grandfathering differs to some extent with the age of men and the way in which fathering and child rearing has been viewed by that generation. Older grandfathers tend to be more formal, in keeping with the masculine father role of their generation, while younger grandfathers are more playful and affectionate. However, there is great variation between individuals.

Grandparents in the news

Not only are there increasing numbers of grandparents as the baby boomers join the grandparent ranks, but in recent years grandparents have been in the news; not front page news perhaps, but as the issues facing grandparents and their contribution to their families has become more obvious, the number of articles in newspapers and magazines is increasing. So what are the issues that have brought grandparents to the notice of the wider community when until the last few years they hardly rated a mention outside family circles?

The first newsworthy concern, and the one most often mentioned, is the role grandparents play in the provision of child care for preschool children and before- and after-school care and holiday care for school-aged children. With many mothers returning to the workforce at least part-time before their children start school, grandparents are often the favoured carers because they provide care in the context of the family. In addition, the shortage of affordable child care places, especially for babies and toddlers, has meant that grandparents have become the major providers of child care for Australian preschool children.

The second matter concerning grandparents that has come to the attention of the media is their contact with grandchildren after their parents separate and/or divorce and also when they re-partner or remarry. In these circumstances many grandparents are anxious about the extent to which their relationship with their grandchildren can be sustained, especially when their own child is not the major carer. During the last 20 to 30 years there has been a great increase in the divorce rate, so this problem has been occurring more frequently.

The third issue, of particular concern for grandparents, and the one which leads to the greatest changes in their lives, is when they have to take full responsibility for the care of grandchildren. Occasionally this is due to the death of the child's parents but more often it happens when the parent has problems with drugs and/or alcohol and this results in the neglect of the grandchildren. Grandparents may take on a parenting role rather than a grandparent role with their grandchildren; this involves great changes in responsibility and finances as well as social and health issues. These three issues for grandparents are addressed in detail in later chapters of the book.

However, when their first grandchild is born these matters are rarely in the minds of grandparents. Rather, they look forward to the pleasures and satisfactions of being grandparents to the next generation in the family.

Becoming a grandparent

Most parents expect and hope to become grandparents, but these days many are concerned that they may never become grandparents as they watch their children growing older without any sign of settling down and having children of their own. This is a reasonable fear, considering the all-time low fertility rate in Australia of 1.75 children per women and an increasing age of parents at the time of the first birth. However, in the last year or so there has been a small increase in fertility figures and this may indicate that the older generation's chances of becoming grandparents are improving. The decision to have a baby, and the timing of this decision, is in the hands of their children and their partners and is something over which the potential grandparents have no control.

When one of their children or daughters-in-law finally becomes pregnant most prospective grandparents look forward to the role. They anticipate the pleasure of getting to know their new grandchild and building a relationship. However, they usually do not expect the extent to which being a grandparent is likely to transform their lives.

With the birth of the first child, both mother and father are aware of enormous changes in identity, in their everyday life, in responsibility, in roles in the household and in their relationship with each other. Becoming a grandparent for the first time, in contrast, does not appear to be such a major change; there is apparently little responsibility and much pleasure to look forward to. Nevertheless, in the human life course becoming a grandparent for the first time is a major life transition. The relationship parents have with their own child and their child's partner changes as they embark on the relationship with the new grandchild.

The following case study provides a picture of this transition from a new grandmother's viewpoint on the birth of her first grandchild. (The name of the grandmother has been changed for confidentiality reasons.)

Rachel

Rachel was at the birth of her first grandchild. She was part of the whole experience well before the baby was born and she and her daughter went shopping for baby things most Saturdays. Because her daughter had decided to use birthing hypnosis for pain management, Rachel also took part in the classes so she could support her at the birth. She photographed the baby girl as she was born and said, 'I felt part of it right from the beginning'.

Rachel's daughter and her partner bought a house about a kilometre away from the family home, so she is able to see the baby four or five times a week and she often visits for half an hour on her way home after work. Although she works full-time her access to her grand-daughter is enhanced by the closeness of her daughter's home and their strong relationship. She is able to have an intimate ongoing relationship with her new grand-daughter.

Rachel says she has a wonderful relationship with 'this new human being'. 'It's an absolute joy and a time when I don't have to think about the stresses of work. There is a sense of future, a sense of hope, a sense of continuity.' She also points out, 'There is no guilt about what you might have done to them, or of missed expectations, and that is really nice.' She loves playing with her grand-daughter and being silly, doing all sorts of things, and watching the baby respond. Rachel and her husband also mind the baby in their home and they have all the necessary equipment—a cot, highchair and pram. She says: 'I don't have to be a disciplinarian, I don't have to be anything but be fun, so when I arrive she rocks her head and throws up her arms and kicks her legs—she's so excited to see me. She loves seeing me.'

Many grandparents, like Rachel, play an important role in the lives of their grandchildren, although only a few attend the birth, while others are more distant and perhaps are grandparents in name only. Grandparents are a diverse group and there are many factors that go beyond personal choice that affect the way in which they grandparent. These factors include the gender of both grandparent and grandchild, whether the grandparent is a maternal or paternal grandparent, the ethnicity and the cultural traditions of the grandparent, the geographic distance between grandparent and grandchild, and whether or not there is any family disruption such as divorce.

Grandparents are also affected by the timing of the births of their grandchildren. There are times that are seen as appropriate for the birth of grandchildren and times that are not. Where children give birth to grandchildren at unexpected times, either too early—perhaps a teenage pregnancy—or too late—when grandparents feel that they are too old or their health is too poor to take an active role—they may not be as delighted as they may have been if they had felt the timing of the birth was more appropriate. The transition to grandparenthood is more difficult for some because they have had no choice in the matter.

The grandparent's career

Grandparents, like parents, go through a period of anticipation during the pregnancy. Many grandparents, like Rachel, look forward eagerly to the birth of a new generation of the family and especially if it is the birth of the first grandchild. They believe that being a grandparent offers the pleasures of parenthood without the responsibilities. What happens in reality, however, may be very different from this expectation.

Grandparents remain parents as well as grandparents and thus have dual roles in their family. It is the grandparent's relationship with the parents of their grandchildren which has the greatest influence on the type of contact and the amount of time that they have with their grandchildren. As the grandparents take up their new role, they will initially feel their way in relation to the new grandchild but also discovering differences in their role with the parents of the new baby, and with their own child in particular. In the past the grandparent has had considerable power and influence over their own child and the relationship has its own history from infancy to adulthood. The dual role of grandparent and parent means that at times the grandparent role may be ambiguous and this can account for some of the diffidence that young parents sometimes display towards grandparents and vice versa. While the grandchild is still a baby—and especially if it is the first grandchild—the parent role, rather than the grandparent role, may be the dominant one as the inexperienced new parents struggle to adjust. Sometimes the grandparents may forget that responsibility for the grandchild lies with the parents, not with the grandparents. New parents may feel very uncertain of themselves and their ability to care for the child. There may also be differences in beliefs about child rearing between the generations that add to the uncertainty of the roles, at least in the beginning.

The role that is played by grandparents is largely dependent on the relationships that they already have with their children and children-in-law. Some Australian research found that:

> Important as grandchildren were, they did not somehow magically transform troubled relationships (between parents and children) into equal, intimate ones. Instead they provided another domain in which long term patterns of the relationship were repeated (de Vaus 1994, p. 161).

Grandparents' relationships with their grandchildren are affected by a number of factors in addition to their relationship with the parent generation as mentioned earlier. The actual relationship with grandchildren may vary from a symbolic one where grandparents and grandchildren meet very rarely, perhaps only at family gatherings, to the other extreme where it may be a primary relationship in which the closeness and affection between grandparent and grandchild are similar to those between parents and children.

Grandparents in Aboriginal families play an important role with grandchildren, as Indigenous children are not seen as the responsibility of the biological parents alone; rather they are regarded as the responsibility of the extended family within the traditional kinship system, where possible, even in urban environments. However, parenting and child rearing in many Indigenous communities is fraught with difficulties due to the loss of the land and culture and to disadvantage of various kinds. Children of the 'stolen generation' often have great difficulty in parenting because they missed out on the warmth and care of their own family and also lost their cultural roots:

> In losing our traditional roles within the family, we have lost our identity. This manifests itself in a number of ways: anger and frustration, low self esteem, loss of confidence and self respect, feelings of isolation and alienation, alcohol and drug abuse, as well as family violence (Sam 1992, p. 3).

Grandmothers often bring up their grandchildren when the parent generation is unable to care for their children safely. In the Indigenous community grandparenting, but especially grandmothering, is guided by their own traditions as well as necessity and is unlikely to follow many of the patterns found in the non-Indigenous population.

The birth of the first grandchild brings with it the status of grandparent without any effort on the part of grandparents, but it is the actions of grandparents in relation to the grandchild that extends the role beyond a purely symbolic one. While the grandparenting role can be influenced by the grandparents' own expectations, wishes and needs, and also whether or not they are still in the workforce, it is largely dependent on the wishes, values and needs of their own child and their child-in-law. Some grandparents may wish for a close and loving relationship with their grandchildren but may be denied the opportunity by their own child and/or their child-in-law. Other grandparents are satisfied with the basic symbolic role, perhaps meeting for birthdays and Christmas, and wish for no closer contact. Where grandparents have more than one family of grandchildren they may have quite different roles and relationships with the different sets of grandchildren.

An influential study of grandparents in the USA (Kornhaber 1996) in the 1970s showed that the grandparent–grandchild bond is influenced by but separate from the parent–child bond and that it is a unique biological, social and spiritual attachment in its own right, providing of course there is the opportunity for the bond to develop. Two-thirds of grandparents reported that they did not want to make the same mistakes with their grandchildren that they had made with their own children.

American researchers have found that differences in grandparent–grandchild relationships can be extensive:

> The relationships can vary from grandchild to grandchild. Some grandchildren may live far from the grandparents, other grandchildren may live with parents who don't get along with the grandparents; still others may no longer be living with the grandparent's son or daughter as a result of divorce. Under circumstances such as these, grandparents sometimes devote most of their attention to a few grandchildren—or even just to one.

This strategy—which we will call selective investment—allows them to act like grandparents and feel satisfied with their role, even though they aren't as close to the rest of the grandchildren (Cherlin & Furstenberg 1985, p. 97).

There are usually significant differences in the feelings that parents have for their own children and the feelings, however loving, that they have for their grandchildren. Grandparents often worry more about their own children and the stresses they are experiencing than about the grandchildren who may be causing the stress. This is not to say that they do not care about the grandchildren, but the grandparents do not have to make the decisions about what to do and they are not responsible for the grandchildren. It is usually much less stressful being a grandparent than being a parent and fearing doing the wrong thing. (The exception is when grandparents have to take over the custodial care of their grandchildren; this will be discussed in Chapter 3.)

From a 'survival of the species' perspective the desire to bond with a new grandchild is an important force. There is a great deal of significance attached to the bonding of mother and child, and to some extent to bonding with the father, but little attention is paid to the grandparents' bonding experience. Attachment and bonding occurs within warm, intimate and continuous relationships and is based on the sensitivity and responsiveness of the adult to the baby. This attachment relationship makes the child feel safe within a secure and predictable relationship. Secure bonds, to mothers in particular, are seen as important to the future development of children but especially to their emotional and social development. Less attention is paid to bonding and relationships with other members of the family, however, children can also form bonds with other members of the family, including grandparents, with whom they have regular positive contact and whose presence makes them feel secure and comfortable. Experts in the field of attachment and security in young children point out that there are advantages in having a relationship with a number of significant adults and see this as the best situation for children. It means that the child has back-up care and the influence of a range of different people on their development.

My own experience as the grandmother of four grandchildren in two families reflects some of these differences. My bonds with my grandchildren, particularly as they get beyond the baby stage, have developed in different ways and have qualities of their own. They are also very different from the bonds and feelings that I had for my own two children; one aspect of this is that I do not have the same responsibility for them. Distance is the major factor which affects my relationship with my grandchildren who live in Tokyo. My daughter's two children live in Melbourne so I can see them more often, although they now live in a suburb which is some distance from where I live. This distance is more easily overcome and we often talk on the phone, so there is more continuity in the relationship. The second factor influencing these relationships is the age difference between the two sets of grandchildren and my own age. Robert and Anne are 12 and 14, while Jack is six and Zoe is three. I was younger and fitter when the older grandchildren were born and in the interim have injured my back. I now have to be careful lifting the younger children and it is more awkward when I take them to a playground. I also get tired more quickly than when I was younger. A third influencing factor is their different personalities. Each one is very different and my relationship with each is unique and some are easier than others. The older grandchildren are bilingual and have had quite different cultural influences in Japan, while the two younger children speak only English and have always lived in the familiar Australian environment. My relationship with each of the children has changed as they have grown older, have developed different interests and have become more independent.

There can be unexpected twists and turns in the grandparent experience. When my first grandchild, Anne, was born I was delighted. She lived with her parents in the same suburb and I looked forward to a close relationship with her. However, when she was four years old and her little brother was only two her parents moved to Tokyo and from that time I could only see her if I went over there or on the occasions when they visited Australia for a holiday. This made it much more difficult to have a close relationship. Children change so much in a few months and what is a relatively short time for adults is a very long time for a child. Each time she visited we had to get to know each other again to some extent. It was fun when I had her and her brother for an excursion when they were in Australia, but it was not very often. When I spent time with them in Japan I was limited in what I could do with them as I do not speak Japanese. Sometimes when I took the children out they would speak Japanese rather than English and I would be left out of parts of the conversation; early on I found that it was very boring watching videos in Japanese! Anne and I still have a good relationship but it is very different from what I had expected at the time of her birth. I have continued to live in the same house in the same suburb, so everything is familiar to Anne and her brother Robert. I have also had the same cat, Pepper, for a long time and she provides a sense of continuity for my grandchildren and they rush to see her when they visit. This year things have changed again. Anne is at boarding school in Australia and I am her guardian. She stays with me when she has weekends away from school, and I have the pleasure of forging a much closer relationship with her. This is my experience; other grandparents will have quite different experiences in their grandparent careers and the twists and turns may be quite unexpected although for some of course little changes except that the grandchildren grow older.

Arthur Kornhaber, who founded the Grandparent Foundation in the United States, believes that the foundations for the way we grandparent come from our personal experience of our grandparents in childhood. He says these experiences lead to a wish for grandchildren of our own when the time is ripe, although this longing may not be fulfilled in all cases. Of course, some parents have not had any experience of grandparents of their own if they died before they were born but this does not prevent them from having ideas and beliefs about grandparenting. Furthermore, not everyone's experience of grandparents is positive, and some grandparents may have to overcome negative childhood experiences. My view is that we add to our ideas about grandparenting by observing the way in which our own parents fulfil the grandparent role with our own children, and what we observe in the behaviour of other grandparents around us.

Grandparenting styles and family involvement

A lot of research has examined the meaning of the grandparent role to grandparents themselves, the dimensions of the role within the family, and the style of the actual relationship with grandchildren. As discussed earlier, the grandparent role is not simply a relationship between grandparents and their grandchildren but is imbedded within the family system and relationships within and between the generations.

Research has found five aspects of the meaning of the role to grandparents. These are:

1 centrality, or the extent to which the role is central to the grandparents' lives

2 valued elder and resource person

3 the feeling of immortality achieved through grandchildren and family continuity (this is particularly important to grandfathers)

4 a sense of reliving personal events in the past and consciously thinking and wondering about their own grandparents

5 indulgence and lenience when catering to the wishes of grandchildren (this is generally more important to grandmothers than grandfathers).

In relation to the family as a whole, four dimensions of being a grand-parent have been suggested and are generally supported by evidence from research:

1 simply 'being there' especially during family transitions and disruptions

2 acting as the 'family watchdog'; there to protect and give care when needed

3 as arbitrators within the family, especially between parents and children

4 sometimes seen by researchers as the most important dimension, as active participants in the family history; grandparents tie the present to the past and also look to the future, thus providing links between the generations.

Styles of relating to grandchildren have received the most research attention. Research as far back as the 1960s found that there were several styles of grandparent–grandchild relationships and these are still relevant today (Neugarten & Weinstein 1964). Descriptions of these styles can provide a framework for grandparents to think about their own dominant style and what is important to them. These styles are closely related to the meanings and overall dimensions of grandparenthood listed above. These are:

- **Formal:** traditional prescribed role that involves some babysitting and indulging of the grandchildren

- **Fun seeker:** these grandparents are informal and playful with the grandchildren (Rachel in the case study of a new grandparent fits into this category)

- **Surrogate parent:** mostly grandmothers who care for grandchildren while the child's parents are working (this also includes grandparents who are bringing up grandchildren and have custodial care)

- **Reservoir of family wisdom:** these grandparents know more about life and family values

- **Distant figure:** contact with grandchildren is infrequent and usually limited to family rituals such as Christmas.

At the time, the researchers found that together the 'Fun seekers' and 'Distant figures' made up 50 per cent of their sample of grandparents. This research took place in the United States, which has a much more mobile population than Australia, and this is likely to have affected the proportion of grandparents who saw themselves in the 'Distant figure' category.

When researchers in Milwaukee County in the United States asked grandparents what they enjoyed most about being a grandparent the responses fell into six categories (Brintnall-Peterson, Rozie-Battle & Nelson 2002). These grandparents most enjoyed:

- unconditional love, with an understanding that love is both received and given

- contact; spending time with grandchildren but with an understanding that they could give them back when they were tired and had had enough

- observing the growth and developmental process, including a sense of renewal and fulfilment from watching over the next generation

- special activities, which included a wide variety of events and special occasions such as family gatherings, and particular outings with grandparents

- being a teacher, listener, historian, advisor and spiritual and emotional confidant (this was seen as a wider role than simply a mentor), and

- finally, a provider. This category included grandparents who were bringing up grandchildren, and other grandparents who were providing support of one sort or another, including financial, for grandchildren.

Generally, grandparents feel that they are making an important contribution to their grandchildren's lives. A recent survey carried out by AARP in the USA of 1500 members who were grandparents indicated that grandparents believe that they are actively sharing a number of child rearing and care-giving roles with parents (Davies 2002). These roles include teaching children values and family history, entertaining them, and listening to their problems. More than two-thirds of these grandparents, aged between 45 and 100 years (with a mean age of 64), see a grandchild every one or two weeks and eight in ten grandparents speak to a grandchild by telephone at least once every couple of weeks. A significant number of the grandparents were helping to support their grandchildren on a day-to-day basis and on average spending about $500 a year on their grandchildren. A little over half reported providing some financial help with their education and 45 per cent with living expenses.

Where grandparents have too much responsibility for grandchildren it has been found that they feel that the 'magical elements' of being able to love and indulge grandchildren can be lost. Many grandparents feel that they lack the authority to take parent-like responsibility with their grandchildren or indeed to tell their own child or their in-law child what to do with grandchildren. American researchers argue that unlike the past where bonds between grandparents, parents and grandchildren were based on economic need and obligation, these days they are based on sentiment and affection but also on 'emotional distance'. In their research they found that American grandparents subscribe to a 'norm of non-interference' and feel that they do not have the right to tell their children what to do with their grandchildren. However, this does not mean that they do not want to do so on occasion! Similar attitudes are commonly found among Australian grandparents, although of course some grandparents do interfere and/or hold forth with their own views.

Other researchers in the United States have found that while the 'norm of non-interference' does indeed exist, that in more connected families non-interference is replaced by 'respectful cooperation' (Kornhaber 1996). Grandparents in this way try to be supportive and nurturing of both parents and grandchildren without being meddlesome, but there is a fine line between constructive criticism and interference. Nevertheless, there are sometimes disagreements between grandparents and parents and these usually focus on differences in child rearing beliefs.

Grandparents can also be a valuable support to children after the separation and divorce of their parents. A study that focused on the emotional adjustment of children in divorced families compared with intact families found that regardless of family status a strong relationship with a grandparent was helpful to a child's social and emotional adjustment. Other studies have found that grandparents have an influence on children's values in regard to such things as religion, politics and attitudes to sex. Studies have generally found that children are closer to their grandmothers, and particularly the maternal grandmother, than to grandfathers.

Grandparents and personal development

Grandparenting has personal aspects for individuals as well as the dimensions associated more directly with their relationships within the family and with their grandchildren. Becoming a grandparent for the first time is a marker of getting older, even though some parents become grandparents at a young age. Some grandparents find it difficult to accept this indication of ageing, at least in the beginning, while others do not seem to mind. For example, I heard a relatively young grandfather refer to his grandchild as his 'daughter's baby' rather than as his grandchild, suggesting that he did not at first identify himself as a grandfather. However, as time passed he began to refer to the child as his grandchild.

The writer of the Mrs Browne trilogy makes the point about age, with some exaggeration, in his entertaining book *The Granny*. He describes 47-year-old Agnes Browne's delight at the birth of her first grandchild until the moment that her son called her 'Granny'!

The word feels like a sack of coal across Agnes's back. She felt her shoulders dip and her spine bend. For some inexplicable reason she hadn't thought about it like that at all. She looked at the back of her left hand—it looked wrinkled and her wedding ring seemed to sink into the flesh of her fourth finger. For the first time in her life Agnes Browne felt old (O'Carroll 2002, p. 15).

On the other hand, grandparents who have been afraid that they were going to miss out on grandchildren are unlikely to be bothered by the suggestion of ageing embodied in the role.

Until recently, most research information on grandparents was found in books on ageing rather than in books on parenting, and indeed the birth of the first grandchild is listed as one of the first indicators of ageing. The links with ageing and mortality may be unwelcome to some parents even when they have other positive feelings about the grandchild as in the case with Agnes Browne. Nevertheless, grandparents are no longer uniformly seen as aged and many become grandparents in early middle age, or even younger, when they are still actively engaged in the workforce. Grandmothers, in particular, may just be coming into their own in regards to employment. These younger grandparents may also have children of their own still at home.

The term 'development' is often applied to children, but frequently it is forgotten that adults continue to develop throughout their whole life. Development in humans of all ages is described as '… a result of interchange between biological processes and environmental influences' and this interchange does not come to a halt after childhood (Kornhaber 1996, p. 56). Grandparenting, like every stage of the life cycle, is developmental. The grandparenting stage of life changes over time not only as grandchildren grow and as the grandparents themselves grow older but it also offers the opportunity for emotional integration and reflection rather than self absorption. Understanding grandparenting as a developmental process provides a way of understanding the diversities in the role as well as the meaning of the role in the life cycle.

Grandchildren develop from infants and toddlers to preschool children, to middle childhood at primary school, to adolescence, and to young adulthood. Along with these developmental changes and challenges, their relationships with their grandparents and their parents alter. However, like parents, grandparents must 'let go' as children grow older, but the extent to which this is necessary will depend to some degree on the role that the grandparents have played in relation to each grandchild. Grandparents may not always be aware of this and may wonder why their grandchildren no longer want to be with them. On the other hand, some grandchildren become closer as they get older and discuss issues with grandparents that they do not want to discuss with their own parents.

Erikson, one of the early psychoanalysts, concerned with the psychological stages of human development, argues that the role of the older mature adult is 'generative' and is concerned with establishing and guiding the next generation. He also pointed out that older mature adults need to be needed and that they need encouragement and guidance from those they care about. Grandparents, who are no longer centre-stage in the family, are also able to reflect on their lives and the lives of the following generations, and to support them with the wisdom of experience and age.

Grandparents and children's development

Children need experiences with adults of all ages, and relationships with older members of their own family provide them not only with greater security but also with an understanding of the human life cycle. Contact between children and grandparents can be helpful and mutually satisfying to both generations provided they have the opportunities to spend time together. Grandparents carry cultural knowledge and knowledge of their own particular family and its heritage that can give their grandchildren a sense of where they belong both in the community and within their extended family. James Hillman, a Jungian psychologist, sums up this aspect of the grandparent role:

> Grandmothers and grandfathers maintain rituals and traditions, possess a hoard of primal stories, teach the young, and nurture the memory of ancestral spirits who guard the community. Grandparents listen to

dreams, and tell you what a new word means; they can tie a fly, bait a hook, and know where the best place is. They live among odd objects, which they cherish, and smells [which are] unforgettable. They have little time left, yet so much time to spare (Hillman 1999, p. 188).

Hillman also argues that, unlike parents, grandparents are not caught up in the daily routines of living with children, and because of this they have a broader view of their grandchild's development and future potential. Grandparents can also afford to be inspired about the child rather than worrying over small and passing things; this aspect of grandparenting is obviously not relevant if grandparents have to take on full-time custodial care of grandchildren. Grandparents usually find their role satisfying and emotionally fulfilling; they gain a sense of personal and family renewal. A grandmother of eight children had this to say about her role:

> I love the kids. I think it's a pleasure to be with the children. I think it enriches the children. I was very distressed that my children didn't have grandparents. My mother died when I was young and I came from Sydney so I didn't have any relatives [in this city]. I always thought that children needed grandparents.

This grandmother enjoys her grandchildren and also provides back-up care for the grandchildren when the parents want to go out or away for the weekend or if the grandchildren are sick when their parents are working.

These days, grandparents are generally viewed by their children, and by researchers, as a resource for the family, particularly when there is a crisis. However, grandparents have not always been seen as having a benign or positive influence on grandchildren. In the 1940s and 1950s grandparents were seen by some clinicians as having a detrimental influence on grand-children by interfering in their upbringing. Research at the time also indicated that the role of grandparent had little significance for older people. Freud, the father of psychoanalysis and modern psychiatry, did not consider the role of grandparents in his theory and practice although it was an important role for him personally. These negative attitudes have changed almost entirely and grandparents are usually viewed positively although, of course, there can at times be conflict between the generations.

Children also see their relationships with their grandparents as changing over time as they develop. Research into children's views of grandparents in the USA has shown that grandparents are important but that their role and value changes as children get older (Kornhaber 1996). When they are very young, before they go to school, children enjoy the indulgent attitudes and behaviour of grandparents; as they get older they have fun with their grandparents; but by the time they are 11 or 12 they prefer some distance in this relationship. Children who had had frequent contact with their grandparents had favourable attitudes, especially to their maternal grandmother, and more than half the children in the study thought that they were important to their grandparents and valued by them.

Most adult grandchildren express affection, respect and fondness for at least one grandparent. They also often expect grandparents to liaise with their parents, to provide personal advice and to understand them. Sometimes grandparents act as role models for grown grandchildren. Of course, grandparents may play different roles with different grandchildren, but it is usually the eldest grandchild who sets the pace in the grandparent's life course.

Conclusions

Although the grandparent's role has become so important in family life over recent years, some current trends in our communities limit children's exposure to grandparents and to older generations in general. The creation of retirement villages for the elderly, and the building of new suburbs for young families, rather than life in integrated communities, limit children's experiences with adults of different ages in their daily lives. Trends such as this contribute also to a reduction of contact between the generations and the support that they provide for each other.

As grandchildren grow up, grandparents age. They may not physically be able to do what they did when the grandchildren were young; they may have health problems, or personal difficulties that have developed over time. While there are many satisfactions in being a grandparent, there can also be worries. Researchers have found five areas of stress and conflict in the grandparent role (Jendrek 1993). These are:

- anxiety about ageing
- tension over the lack of control involved in being a grandparent
- competition with other members of the family, including the other set of grandparents and the parents
- pressure to relinquish the comfort of retirement (if the grandparents are no longer in employment) and to assume responsibility for the care of the grandchildren, and
- tension from personal factors.

Grandparents have also reported a strain between their own expectations of what grandparenting would be like and the way it actually turned out. These areas of stress and conflict will be discussed throughout this book. They do not always lead to crises but arise in the ongoing intergenerational relationships among family members. On the other hand there are sometimes crises—such as divorce, or the excessive use of drugs and alcohol by parents—which can result in heartache for those concerned, and these will also be discussed.

There are other sources of concern for grandparents. Grandparents may be thought of as experienced in child rearing, having brought up their own children; nevertheless, they may have beliefs about child rearing and values which are different from the parents and/or out-of-step with current beliefs about child rearing. These days there is great concern about parenting and also with the rights of the child. Parents themselves are expressing the need to learn more about parenting, and parenting classes are increasingly available and often seen as necessary. An understanding of child development and behaviour management is an important part of these courses. Despite the fact that many grandparents are major carers of their grandchildren there is little support provided for them in this role and little to specifically inform them about current attitudes and expectations about child rearing except through the media. While this is changing to some extent, with playgroups available for some grandparents and grandchildren, and the occasional parenting or grandparenting group, these are far from readily available.

The following chapters cover the major issues relating to grandparents: providing child care; custodial grandparenting; issues of divorce and remarriage including legal issues relating to grandparent access; issues in child development and behaviour management that grandparents may need to be aware of; and grandparenting children in unusual circumstances such as children with special needs, and grandchildren of lesbian and gay couples, and finally, the death of a grandchild.

References

Baydar, N & Brooks-Gunn, J 1991, *Profiles of American grandmothers: those who provide care for their grandchildren and those who do not*, Seattle Population Research Centre Working Paper No. 11.

Bourke, E 1993, 'The first Australians: kinship, family and identity', *Family Matters*, no. 35, pp. 4–6.

Brintnall-Peterson, M, Rozie-Battle, J & Nelson, C 2002, 'Milwaukee County Grandparent Research', Fact Sheet, University of Wisconsin Extension.

Cadd, M 1999, 'Indigenous Australians: a new deal for a new century?', ACOSS Papers 105, selected papers from the 1999 ACOSS Congress, Strawberry Hills.

Cherlin, A & Furstenberg, F 1985, 'Styles and strategies of grandparenting', in VL Bengtson, & JF Robertson (eds), *Grandparenthood*, Sage, Beverly Hills, pp. 97–116

Davies, C 2002, *The Grandparent Study 2002 report*, AARP, US, viewed 6 April 2006, (www.aarp.org/research/family/grandparenting/aresearch-import-481.html).

De Vaus, D 1994, *Letting go: relationships between adults and parents*, OUP, Melbourne.

Erikson, EH 1950, *Childhood and society*, Penguin, Harmondsworth.

Glezer, H 1991, 'Cycles of care between generations', *Family Matters*, no. 30, pp. 44–6.

Hagestad, G 1985, 'Continuity and connectedness', in VL Bengtson, & JF Robertson (eds), *Grandparenthood*, Sage, Beverly Hills, pp. 31–48.

Hillman, J 1999, *The force of character*, Random House, Sydney.

Jendrek, M 1993, 'Grandparents who parent their grandchildren: effects on lifestyle', *Journal of Marriage and the Family*, vol. 55, pp. 609–21.

King, V & Elder, G 1997, 'The legacy of grandparenting: childhood experiences with grandparents and current involvement with grandchildren', *Journal of Marriage and the Family*, vol. 59, no. 4, pp. 848–60.

Kornhaber, A 1996, *Contemporary grandparenting*, Sage, Thousand Oaks.

Lewis, RA 1990, 'The adult child and the older parents', in TH Brubaker (ed.), *Family relationships in later life*, Sage, Newbury Park, pp. 68–85.

McGreal, CE 1994, 'The family across generations: grandparenthood', in L L'Abate (ed.), *Handbook of developmental psychology and psychopathology*, Wiley-Interscience Publication, New York, pp. 116–31.

Millward, C 1994, 'Intergenerational family support: help or hindrance', in *Family Matters*, no. 39, pp. 10–13.

Neugarten, B & Weinstein, K 1964, 'The changing American grandparent', *Journal of Marriage and the Family*, vol. 26, pp. 199–204.

O'Carroll, B 2002, *The granny*, Penguin, Camberwell.

Perlmutter, M & Hall, E 1992, *Adult attachment and aging*, John Wiley and Sons, New York.

Rice, PL 1994, *Asian mothers, Australian birth*, Ausmed Publications, Melbourne.

Roberto, K 1990, 'Grandparent and grandchild relationships', in TH Brubaker (ed.), *Family relationships in later life*, 2nd edn, Sage, Newbury Park, pp. 100–12.

Rossi, A 1993, 'Intergenerational relations: gender, norms and behaviour', in VL Bengtson, & W Achenbaum (eds), *The changing contract across generations*, Aldine De Gruytor, New York, pp. 191–211.

Ruoppila, I 1991, 'The significance of grandparents for the formation of family relations', in PK Smith (ed.), *The psychology of grandparenthood: an international perspective*, Routledge, London, pp. 123–42.

Sam, M 1992, *Through black eyes*, Secretariat of National Aboriginal and Islander Child Care, Fitzroy, Vic.

Simpson, JA & Rholes, WS (eds) 1998, *Attachment theory and close relationships*, The Guilford Press, New York.

Tavecchio, L & van IJzendoorn, M 1987, *Attachment in social networks: contributions to the Bowlby-Ainsworth attachment theory*, North Holland, Amsterdam.

Troll, L 1980, 'Grandparenting', in L Poon (ed.), *Aging in the 1980s: psychological issues*, American Psychological Association, Washington, pp. 475–81.

Troll, L 1985, 'The contingencies of grandparenting', in VL Bengtson, & JF Robertson (eds), *Grandparenthood*, Sage, Beverly Hills, pp. 135–49.

Weston, R 1992, 'Families after marriage breakdown', *Family Matters*, no. 32, pp. 41–5.

Weston, R, Qu, L & Soriano, G 2003, 'Australia's ageing yet diverse population', *Family Matters*, no. 66, pp. 6–13.

Whitbeck, I, Hoyt, D & Huck, S 1993, 'Family relationship history, contemporary parent–grandparent relationship quality, and the grandparent–grandchild relationship', *Journal of Marriage and the Family*, vol. 55, no. 4, pp. 1025–35.

Chapter 2

Child care, babysitting, and time with grandchildren

Most grandparents enjoy time with their grandchildren, taking them out to playgrounds, on various other excursions, and having them in their own homes for visits and sometimes for sleepovers. Almost all grandparents, if they live close enough to their grandchildren, spend time with them. Even those who live far away try to see their grandchildren and keep in contact unless they have a bad relationship with the parents. Babysitting and taking care of grandchildren for short periods while parents have appointments or other business to attend to is also something that many grandparents do and that grandparents have always done. What is new in the last ten to fifteen years is the more widespread provision of child care by grandparents, particularly for babies and toddlers. When both parents are in the workforce, grandparents are now the biggest providers of child care for children under 12 years of age in Australia. This is also true in many other countries. Providing child care for grandchildren is one of the issues that has brought grandparents to the attention of the media; issues related to grandparents caring for grandchildren feature regularly on radio and television, and in newspapers and magazines.

Grandmothers do most of the caring for grandchildren, but grandfathers also play a role. Grandfathers often find their time with grandchildren especially satisfying because they feel they are making up for their unavailability, due to work pressures, when their own children were young. One of the grandfathers I interviewed puts it this way:

I can't remember doing anything with my kids. I never played with them. I never had the time when I was on the land. I honestly cannot remember playing with them at all. I get a lot of enjoyment out of the grandkids.

Another grandfather who is still a busy professional and has had a similar experience puts it somewhat differently:

I'm more in the space with my grandchildren than perhaps I was with my own children. It's been a very different experience because there are huge slabs of [time when] my kids [were] growing up that I can't recall now. My wife says that I was great, that I was around, but I can't remember. I think that I can be in a space with my grandchildren now—a very different space than when I was a parent. Lots of my friends have said that to me as well. I think the reason for me is that when you have your own kids you're externally focused. You are making your way in the world, you're building a career, looking for approval, so you are physically with your kids but you are externally focused. I think with being a grandparent you know your place in the world. You know who you are. I'm much more internally focused. I can be with my grandchildren in a space that I can't recall ever being with my own kids. My son has said to my wife. 'I love the way Dad is with B [grandson]. He wasn't like that with me.'

This may be true also for some grandmothers but is more likely with grandfathers.

A number of case studies of grandparents are used in this chapter to illustrate the differences between spending time with grandchildren, including babysitting, and providing child care. The case studies illustrate the satisfaction that many grandparents find in their relationships with their grandchildren, the different approaches and situations involved, and to some extent the different family styles and networks. They also demonstrate the responsibilities involved in providing child care. In families where there is more than one set of grandchildren the grandparents may be playing quite different roles with each family. The names of the grandparents in these case studies have been changed for reasons of confidentiality. Grandmothers took part more often than grandfathers usually because they were easier to contact and were more willing to be interviewed, but also because more often than not they are the ones that spend more time with their grandchildren. Some case studies also provide some information about broader family relationships including the role of the other set of grandparents.

Some grandparents see providing child care as their role and responsibility and even their pleasure, while others are less convinced, even though they may be involved in child care provision. A number of grandparents are quite clear that they are not willing to provide child care, although they may babysit, spend time with and are concerned about and interested in their grandchildren. The following case studies are of grandparents who do not provide child care although they are very involved with their grandchildren; it is followed by a contrasting section about grandparents who provide child care. The similarities and differences in the two situations are made clear in the comparison.

Time spent with grandchildren

Many grandparents do not provide child care but still have regular and close relationships with their grandchildren and some still have a great deal of responsibility. The following three case studies demonstrate the rich and varied relationships between grandparents and grandchildren and some of the things that they do together. The third case study is of a grandmother who is extremely pressured by her family circumstances.

Beth and James

James and Beth are in their mid-sixties and are in a second marriage of many years duration. James has three children and Beth has one daughter. James' eldest daughter and her husband have three children aged 8, 5 and 3 years and live reasonably close to the grandparents. This daughter is the only one of the four children who lives in Australia. Beth's daughter has no children but James' other two children, a son and a daughter, have two children each.

Beth is quite clear about their grandparenting role: 'I think that we are grandparents who set boundaries around grandparenting.' She explains:

> *Theoretically having children enriches you and the same applies to grand-*
> *children. In reality a few hours a week is enough being with them because*
> *basically I'm not a child-oriented person. I like being adult doing adult things.*
> *So after a few hours I feel like I want to turn off childish things.*

However, this statement belies the amount of time spent with her grandchildren and the effort that she and James put into their time with them.
James explains:

> *What I like about being a grandparent is that those little kids have 25 per*
> *cent of my DNA. It's nice to know that some of your DNA is going to be*
> *wandering around. But that's a theoretical sort of construct. Beth and I are*
> *quite compatible in our feeling towards the grandchildren; both of us get*
> *rather bored and impatient. In theory I love it, I think it's a great thing to*
> *do, and they are cute, but after an hour or two we start getting very itchy*
> *and going up the wall. That's why the afternoon thing where we meet them*
> *at the playground and I go with the boys and take them there for an hour and*
> *our grand-daughter does her tennis lesson suits us well. On the other hand,*
> *I suppose it is part of my own nature that I have a certain amount of ability*
> *to turn off and be a bit childish. In the swimming pool with them I am quite*
> *happy and I really enjoy it. We took them kite flying a few weeks ago which I*
> *also enjoy. It's different. On the whole I share the same sort of general feeling*
> *[as Beth]—I get bored and frustrated if we spend too much time. At the same*
> *time I feel that there is something rewarding about a certain amount of time.*
> *In theory it is very good but in practice it has some limitations.*

Beth has many interests other than grandchildren and is doing some volunteer
work now that she is retired:

> *I think that I enjoy them more when it's just part of a busier life that has nothing*
> *to do with children. When we babysit on a Sunday from 5.30 p.m. we make them*
> *dinner, play with them, read to them, and put them to bed—2 hours and that's*
> *just right. Being around children and childish things has never been the most*
> *satisfying part of being the person I am. I enjoy it for short periods of time.*

James and Beth do not see themselves as child care providers although they
have the children for a day a week in the school holidays. Mostly they spend

time with the grandchildren as a couple as that makes it easier with three children involved:

> *I think we made a deliberate decision, given our temperaments, and we have never offered to have the children for one day a week. We talk about it, and think it would be a great thing to do, and we do feel guilty when other people talk about doing it. However, for us selfishness seems to over-ride guiltiness. We talk about it and say we could pick the kids up one afternoon a week and that would be a help but unless we are required we don't do it.*

As the grandchildren get older Beth enjoys them more because she can do things with then that she likes doing too. Beth says:

> *I really don't like babies. We are looking forward to them getting older and doing more mature things with them but also we're scared to death about what they are going to be like when they are older.*

Despite this James says babies just love Beth because she gives them all her attention. He is also worried about when they become teenagers because 'they can be very difficult too and I'm not a very great disciplinarian'.

James and Beth are also firm in their decision not to care for the grandchildren if they are ill because they usually catch whatever the children have and get it much worse than the children. 'If they had measles or chicken pox that would be fine but we often get our colds and 'flu from the kids so if they are really sick we say sorry, no.' However, when the grandchildren's mother was in the hospital for quite a long period they cared for the older two children every day for a few hours. They picked them up from crèche at about 3.30 p.m., took them to visit their mother and often gave them dinner. They said that under the circumstances they would have done more but the grandchildren's father said that he was handling it fine. On the other hand Beth believes that the parents could call on them a bit more, for example, if they have a doctor's appointment. She thinks they may hesitate because they are aware of their views about child minding.

The grandchildren who do not live in Australia are visited for about four days each year. Beth has tried to think of ways to keep connected to them. She comments:

I do what I can do because I believe it is important. When we visited the newest baby their mother had put photos of us all over the fridge to make sure that the children would recognise us. I was very touched by her doing that although she doesn't communicate from one year to the next. We are particularly lucky that with all this benign neglect of the grandchildren the parents seem quite happy when we come and spend time with them.

Beth also has a special bond with them all through the quilts she has made for them. All the grandchildren really love the quilts. She also writes them letters which she decorates with little paintings she does of Australian birds and animals and other little figures.

Leon (and Kate)

Leon and Kate, who are in their early sixties, are professionals with satisfying careers. They have two grandchildren, the children of their son and his wife, and their daughter is about to give birth to their third grandchild. Their grandson who is aged four-and-a-half attends kindergarten, and their grand-daughter is aged two and is in crèche for two days a week as her mother works part-time. The family is Jewish. Both children and the grandchildren live only about 20 minutes by car away from the grandparents so they are able to see a lot of them and they will also be able to see the new grandchild easily after it is born. Leon and Kate do not provide child care but they spend lots of time with their grandchildren. Leon says: 'Kate is a career woman and she likes to work,' but they see their grandchildren every week and their grandson spends at least one night with them. As their grand-daughter gets older she is also starting to spend a night regularly. The grandparents sometimes babysit the grandchildren in the evening and usually ask if they can come to their house earlier in the afternoon so that they can spend more time with them while they are awake.

Leon describes how he feels about his grandchildren:

It's not even babysitting, there is nothing I would rather do than look after the grandchildren. When my wife and daughter went away for the weekend recently I had my grandson for the weekend from Friday night to Sunday night. I had two nights! We caught a tram and visited two art galleries, we went on a Ferris wheel, we made scones, we read books, and we kicked the football around. On the Sunday my son called and asked if I could babysit his sister that afternoon but I said no because I didn't want to dilute my experience with my grandson. It was just a very special time. I felt a little guilty! There is nothing I would rather do than have time with him, it's just such a joy.

Leon feels at four-and-a-half his grandson is a good companion.

I'm very conscious that my very special relationship is with the first [grandchild]. With his sister I am conscious of having to make a bit of an effort although she is gorgeous. Kate [the grandmother] is more bonded to our grand-daughter now than I am but she was the same. I'm conscious that with my daughter's child, I will have to make an effort. I think that the first is always very special. I saw him about an hour after birth and it was so precious I wept.

Leon never knew grandparents:

My parents are Holocaust survivors. All their families were wiped out. My mother lost three sisters and my father lost brothers and sisters. I came to Australia when I was three so I never knew my grandparents. I was born in Kazakhstan in a labour camp. My mother had had a child before me that died and so I was a precious baby for her. I had a brother as well. So I never knew grandparents, and seeing the way my children related to my parents as they grew up gave me such pleasure. Both of them had very strong connections with my parents. My daughter had a really special bond with my mother. When she was in her early teens if she had been away for the weekend or even a day she would say 'Hi' to us and walk straight to the phone to call her grandmother. It was a huge comfort to my parents who had lost so many relatives.

The next generation is so important; it's part of the Jewish culture. I don't know if this is just post-Holocaust. There's a treasuring and a celebration of the next generation. In a way it's in defiance of Hitler. I think Jewish families are suffocating, over-close, and so on, but so are Italian, Greek and Turkish families. It's a European, Mediterranean thing as opposed to the Anglo approach which is much more reserved. I think in Jewish families there is more physical touching. If my grandson stays overnight he gets kissed at least 50 times. He is always hugged and kissed. He is very close to both sets of grandparents. He's very special.

> The other set of grandparents are Jewish too. They live even closer to their grandchildren than Leon and Kate do, and are very involved as well. The other grandfather picks up their grandson from kinder every day. Recently, the parents went away for three weeks and both sets of grandparents worked together to care for the grandchildren. Both grandchildren stayed with Leon and Kate and they dropped them off at kinder and crèche in the morning. The other grandparents picked them up in the afternoon and gave them dinner. Leon or Kate then picked them up on the way home and they stayed with them for the night. Leon says: 'These children are grandparented a lot'.

The following case study is one with much food for thought not only about the role of grandparents but also about the ongoing career of grandparents in relation to more than one set of grandchildren and family circumstances that change over time. It provides a much broader picture of the dilemmas that some grandparents face and how grandparenting is part of a much greater web of family relationships. It also shows the pressures that can be placed on grandparents, but especially grandmothers, both by their children, and also by the broader society. This case study also sets the scene for the following chapter where grandparents have responsibility for bringing up grandchildren. Whether this happens to Patricia, the grandmother in this case study, remains to be seen but it hangs over her head and worries her a great deal. She also feels guilty although she does a great deal for her grandchildren.

Patricia

> Patricia, at 53, is one of the younger grandmothers. She was married at nineteen and had two children by the time she was 21. She is divorced and has two sons and three grandchildren and is still paying off her home. Her eldest son has a nine-year-old boy and a six-year-old girl; her younger son has a two-year-old girl. She came from a large family and her youngest brother is only 12 months older than her eldest son. Patricia has a responsible management job which involves a lot of time away from home and interstate travel.
>
> When her eldest grandson was born Patricia was only 45. She was there at the birth and was really excited about it. But one of the things that happened

after the baby was born, and that she found really stressful, was that his mother always wanted Patricia to mind him. Patricia wanted to be around her grandson but she did not want to have to mind him all the time. His parents liked to go out to parties and wanted Patricia to have him overnight. 'But he was one of those crying, highly-strung kind of babies.' He wouldn't settle for anyone but his mother so Patricia was often up all night and would end up in tears herself. This has been an ongoing strain. Patricia explains:

> I want to see my grandchildren, and I want to see them regularly, but I don't want to have the responsibility to look after them. I feel very strongly about that. I don't want to have my grandchildren every weekend and all weekend. I feel there is no time for me at the moment. I get half a day on a weekend for me and that's it.

The expectation that grandparents should always be available to mind grandchildren is a big issue for Patricia:

> There is a perception with young people that because they have a baby that you [the grandmother] are automatically going to be there to mind the child. If you don't you feel guilty. I think that's an awful position for grandparents to be in. I've got lots of friends my age—I'm 53 now—and all of them love their grandchildren and want to see them but they don't want to mind them all the time. They feel guilty if they say no, and it's a real dilemma. Probably it's because I'm working still. If I was home all day I probably would have them more. But I think I would do it because I thought I should rather than because I really wanted to.

At first Patricia could not think what being a grandmother meant to her but then explained how her own experience of her grandmother as a child coloured her view:

> I had a good grandmother and I was really close to her and I used to go and stay with her in the school holidays sometimes. A grandmother, to me, is about having someone that you do special things with and you have a lovely time and you get away with murder basically.

Her own experience as a grandmother is very different. Both her sons are in difficult situations and are separated from their wives. The younger son and his wife, who have a two-year-old daughter, both have mental health problems and are separated because of these. Her daughter-in-law, the mother of the older grandchildren, still wants Patricia to mind the children every weekend.

Patricia's mother and father, on the other hand, never expected to mind grandchildren:

> I remember when my older sister got married and had two children and wanted Mum and Dad to mind the children while they went out. Mum and Dad said that they wouldn't do it, that it was not their job. They still had children of their own at home. Their view was if you've got kids you stay at home and look after them.

Patricia's younger son was diagnosed with paranoid schizophrenia and he has had problems for a long time. His partner has bi-polar disorder. They have a two-year-old daughter who is of great concern to Patricia. Last year was a particularly difficult year. Child Protection Services got involved in the situation, although Patricia now believes that it was a good thing, because her son has now been fully diagnosed and is on proper medication. This has led to great improvements in his wellbeing although he will never be able to live with his partner and his daughter because he is too high a risk. Patricia explained that the parents did well while the child was a baby but as soon as she started moving around it all got too much for the mother. As a result of the parents' difficulties, Patricia cares for her two-year-old grand-daughter every Saturday. Her son has supervised access during that time as he is not allowed to be with her by himself. The two older grandchildren often come over too. A saving grace is that the little girl is very placid although she is 'a bright little button'. This child has a mixture of care during the week. She has two days of child care and is cared for by a range of family members including her mother the rest of the time. Patricia says: 'She's very secure with us and her personality is a huge saving grace because she is very easy going and she's not highly strung'. Nevertheless, Patricia worries about her safety and security when she is in her mother's care because of her unpredictable emotional state:

> It's a constant battle. Do I give up work? How can I be around more because my job takes me all over the place. So I get guilty all the time about what role

I should play and she's more important than anything else. But if I don't work I don't have a house. I can't give up work, and I don't want to give up work. I really like my work and it's interesting because I'm in the field where we talk about how the service system can support families who are in difficulties with child rearing. However, the system as it is set up is not going to be able to protect my grand-daughter. The only people that are going to be able to protect her are family members—that is, the grandparents and the aunts.

Her older grandchildren are a worry in a different way. They are difficult to manage and when they come over:

They look in all the cupboards and go to the fridge as if it's their right to. If you take them somewhere they want you to buy them something all the time and they are used to doing what they want. They are quite hard to look after. You can think these kids should be toeing the line but that doesn't work either.

Her daughter-in-law works full-time and her own mother minds the children when they are not at school. Patricia says that the children are at the other grandmother's place more than at their own home.

Patricia worries about her grandchildren because they are all in difficult situations but she knows that she has to accept things the way they are. She tries to be there for them when she can but her work makes that difficult. 'Trying not to feel guilty about working is one of the biggest issues with me'. She asks: 'Why do I feel guilty though? Why don't I want to have the grandchildren all the time?'

The grandchildren are not the only issue for Patricia as she is one of the 'sandwich generation' caught between the needs of her own children and grandchildren and an ageing parent. Patricia's mother is now 91 and lives in another state. Although she had seven children she is closest to Patricia, who does the most for her despite her busy life. She says:

I phone her up every week and I make sure that she has what she needs because she is just in public housing. I replaced her TV when it was on the blink and so on. They are the little things that I can do. I was trying to bring her over here twice a year for four to five weeks for a holiday so she could see the grandkids.

Her vision is not good now and last time she came I realised that she needs assistance to fly now, otherwise she's quite fit and lives on her own. This year I flew over there for Mother's Day, because she hasn't been well. I hired a car and took her out. She loved that. I worry about what is going to happen when she can't look after herself but none of my siblings are in a position to take her in. I don't know what will happen. I often fancy I will get a house with a granny flat. She doesn't want to go into a nursing home and that's my view about me too. I don't know that I could sit by and let my mother go into a nursing home. I think I would feel so guilty I just couldn't. It's that feeling of being responsible. In terms of my youngest grand-daughter [whose parents both suffer from mental illness] there is no way I could let her go to foster care. I would give up my job tomorrow. She would be truly stuffed if she went to foster care. If I had to take six months leave, I'd do anything, I wouldn't let her go to foster care. I'd hire a nanny; I'd do something. Whatever it took! And with my mother I guess it's similar in a way. I couldn't see her go into a nursing home. She could come and stay with me. The trouble is when she gets to a stage of not being able to care for herself. What's the choice? The choice is for her to go into a nursing home. I couldn't bear that. When something happens and the time comes I will decide. I'm on my own so I can do whatever I like. I can sell my house and buy something else. I don't know.

These three case studies provide some contrasts. Patricia is in the most difficult position and has the most pressures on her, especially as a lone grandmother, but she is not unique; there are many grandparents who are also pressured by family circumstances. The other two sets of grandparents have more comfortable relationships within the family and have not experienced guilt from excessive expectations and difficult circumstances, in the way that Patricia has. None of these grandparents provide child care for their grandchildren but all are doing an enormous amount for their children and grandchildren.

Like the grandparents in the case studies above I did not provide child care for my grandchildren, partly because neither my daughter nor daughter-in-law were in the workforce when their children were little, whereas I worked full-time. I have always been happy to babysit and enjoy taking the children on excursions or to the playground but I have never wanted to provide child care.

However, grandparenting is not only a role but a 'career' which extends over time, as was discussed in Chapter 1. Grandparent 'careers' may be at different stages for the different families of grandchildren depending on their age and what is happening in their family. My role as a grandmother changed recently when my daughter returned to work part time. Her eldest child (aged six) is now at primary school and her daughter (aged three) is in long day preschool for the three days that she works. Her husband has flexible working hours and can pick up the children at the end of each school and preschool day and I am the back-up person for emergencies. In this role I have cared for my three-year-old grand-daughter on days when nobody has been available to care for her and especially in the school holidays. I am happy to do this now as my time is now more flexible and the child care has only been for single days at a time. It is much the same as taking as taking her out on an excursion except that she comes to my house and I have her for a much longer time.

The limitations of my care are now physical compared with when my older grandchildren were little, as I am older and have various old injuries which have returned to plague me. But writing is flexible work so I can find the time! There are two things motivating me in the decision to mind my grand-daughter. The first is to help my daughter out in her new job and the second is because I love Zoe, who is a very sweet, good-natured child. I enjoy having her with me but I get quite tired by the end of the day. But most importantly, I also know that my daughter is aware of my limitations and will not ask too much of me. Grandparenting is not static and grandparents can experience many changes in their roles and relationships with grandchildren as changes occur in their families over time.

Grandparents providing child care

Grandchildren these days are growing up in a society where many families need two incomes, not just for luxuries, but for many of the necessities of everyday life, and especially to pay the mortgage on the family home. With a better educated population there are also more career women who want to return to their work because of commitment to a satisfying occupation. When fewer mothers were in the workforce it was unusual for grandparents to provide child care. In those days most women remained at home after the birth of a child, at least until the children went to school, and to a large degree it was frowned upon for women with preschool children to work. That was certainly my experience when I had young children. Leaving children in the care of others while mothers worked was generally acceptable only in cases where necessity forced them to earn a wage. This state of affairs has changed gradually since the 1970s and has gained much greater momentum in the 1990s.

These days many mothers return to the workforce before their children start school, although most work part-time. Often child care is needed for a few hours especially while the children are babies or toddlers. Changes in the workplace participation of mothers have led to an increase in the use of both the formal child care system and informal care in the home. Formal child care for preschool children is provided outside the family home in child care centres, although family day care is provided in the homes of the care providers. Family day care is often preferred for younger children and babies because it is in a home setting and there are only a small number of children involved. Some parents may leave their children for short time periods of a few hours of occasional care in a child care centre, neighbourhood house or in a leisure centre while they attend classes or have an appointment. In 2002, 45 per cent of children aged up to four years spent some time in formal child care, but it was often for very short periods of time.

Care is provided for school-aged children in after-school care, before-school care and holiday programs or vacation care, and is usually available on school premises, but is sometimes provided in community centres and other venues. In 2002, 13 per cent of children aged five to 11 years spent some time in this type of formal child care (Australian Bureau of Statistics 2002). Formal child care services are licensed by the State and accredited by the Commonwealth governments and must meet certain standards.

Informal child care is provided in the home by relatives (mostly grand-parents but sometimes fathers and aunts), nannies, and in some countries—but rarely in Australia—by au pairs. Informal care is used most often for children under twelve months of age. Informal care is not licensed and the choice of these informal care options depends on what is available, how much it costs, and the parents use their judgment of what best suits them and their child. Nannies are expensive and it is often difficult to find someone who is reliable and affordable. Grandparents are favoured because they are reliable, loving, are part of the family, known by the child and they usually cost nothing or very little. It is easy to understand why grandparents are the principal providers of child care, particularly for preschool children, not only in Australia but in many other countries including the United Kingdom and the United States.

While work commitments are the main reason given for child care by grandparents, most parents also believe that it is good for their children. The younger the child when the mother returns to the workforce the more likely it is that they will be in the care of grandparents. The Australian Bureau of Statistics has found that of children under twelve months of age, 22 per cent were cared for regularly by their grandparents and only seven per cent of children in this age group were in formal day care. For children aged one year, 57 per cent were using some form of child care with grandparents providing 31 per cent of the care. However the majority of preschool children, particularly those under three years, were in child care for relatively short periods of time. Many parents use a mixture of formal and informal care, often by grandparents. The use of grandparent care and other informal care decreases and the use of formal child care in child care centres and family day care increases as children get older. By the time children are four years old, 83 per cent are in formal care but some of this includes attendance at preschools. Parents often feel that as children get older they will benefit from mixing with other children, and so they move the children from informal care to the formal child care system.

Over the years, as the numbers of grandparents providing child care have increased, there have been many studies examining the way in which grandparents experience this role and how it fits into their lives. Many of the studies have been in the United States, partly because it has a bigger population which goes through these demographic trends slightly ahead of Australia, and partly because researchers in that country have greater access to research funds. Much of the information in this chapter draws on research from the United States and the United Kingdom but where possible

Australian research is cited. The issues in these other English-speaking countries are, however, very similar to those in Australia.

Why is grandparent care so popular with parents? A number of Australian studies found that the main reason for the choice of grandparents as carers in a wide range of families from different backgrounds, including culturally and linguistically diverse families, is that they are trusted and mothers feel that this form of care suits the child's needs. Parents want affectionate carers for their children, especially for younger children. Mothers tend to feel less guilt and to worry less when they return to the workforce if their younger children are cared for by their own parents or parents-in-laws rather than in formal child care. Most mothers view grandparent care as the nearest thing to parental care, however this is not true of all mothers. Some prefer the formal system of care, if they can get a place for their child, because they do not feel obligated and they know that the care is of a certain standard and is reliable.

The second major reason for grandparent care is affordability. Formal child care, especially centre-based care, is expensive and although the Federal government provides a means-tested Child Care Benefit to assist with the fees it does not cover the full cost of care, even for low income families, and many families cannot afford the cost. Family day care is less expensive than centre-based care, but is still beyond the financial capacity of many families. In contrast, very few grandparents are paid.

However, even when parents can manage the financial burden of formal child care, it is often difficult to find a place. Although the number of places for preschool children in both centre-based care and family day care have increased over recent years there are still insufficient places for the number of children needing care. There are long waiting lists and it can be very difficult to find places for children when the time comes for mothers to return to work. It is even more difficult to find places for babies and toddlers, as many child care centres do not provide for children under three years of age. It also is becoming increasingly difficult to obtain places in family day care in many areas because it is difficult to find people who want to provide care in their own homes.

The current situation in the formal child care system adds to the pressure on grandparents to provide child care and this is particularly so if the mother returns to the workforce before her youngest child is three. But even where grandparents are not providing regular child care for their grandchildren, they often fill the gaps. Many grandparents pick up children from child care centres, family day care and preschool, they also pick up older children from school, and sometimes from after-school care, and care for them until their parents come home from work. Grandparents help out on curriculum days when parents cannot get time off from work; they sometimes, but not always, step in when children are sick and take over during school holidays for at least part of the time. Some grandparents also care for children when parents go away on holiday breaks.

Grandparent care is dependent on the relationship between the grandparents and the parents, particularly between the mother and the grandmother who tends to do most of the care, and on general goodwill all around. On occasion, of course, grandparent care may be necessary even when there is not a particularly good relationship because there is no other choice and financial necessity forces parents and grandparents into the situation. With older grandparents it may also depend on their health and fitness; some simply may not be able to provide care because they are unwell. For example, one grandmother who had provided child care for her eldest grandchild was unable to do so when her younger daughter had a child because she had occasional dizzy spells which would have been dangerous for the baby.

Some time ago, I had the opportunity to speak with a group of grandparents who were generally either providing some child care or picking up grandchildren after school or from child care. Like me, they found these roles satisfying because they were helping their children and they also enjoyed having time with their grandchildren. However they had two complaints, one about the grandchildren and the other about the parents. The first complaint was that they found it difficult caring for more than one grandchild at a time, partly because of the different developmental ages and partly because they fought and this made it difficult for the grandparents. One child was not a problem, though. The second complaint was that they hardly saw their own children although they were caring for their grandchildren. The parents came in from work tired, grabbed the children and headed for home. They usually had no time to spend with the grandparents (their own parents) and rarely stopped to have a cup of coffee and talk for a bit. This was especially difficult when the grandparents felt they were doing something for their children, not just their grandchildren, although they also understood that time is a big issue.

Taking on responsibility for child care gives some grandparents a purpose in life and a great deal of satisfaction, while others have mixed feelings if they feel the strain of expectations that go beyond what is comfortable and within their capabilities.

The four case studies below are of grandparents who are providing some child care. Some stresses are apparent but the satisfactions are also obvious. These case studies provide food for thought and are followed by a discussion of research on issues relating to grandparents providing child care.

Sandy (and Peter)

Sandy is 57 and has three children. Her middle daughter has two children, a boy of 18 months and a girl just three weeks old. She says: 'I've always loved little kids. I think they're gorgeous. I wasn't planning to become a grandmother (at the time), but now they're here both of them are just the sweetest little things. I'm biased.'

Her daughter works part-time in her husband's family businesses. She went back to work when the first child was about three months old for a couple of days a week. Sandy cared for her grandson one day a week in his own home starting at about 7 a.m. and finishing around 3 p.m. The other grandmother had the child on the second day. However the other grandmother is not as confident with the child and does not feel as physically capable as Sandy. Sandy cares for her grandson in his own home as it is easier to have him where he has his own cot and his own toys. She has found that it is a very 'full-on' day and that it wears her out but she has the convenience of being able to do the shopping on the way home. Sandy also commented that she had wanted her own mother to care for her kids rather than her husband's mother, although she was a lovely motherly woman.

Sandy's daughter plans to go back to work part-time two days a week when the second grandchild is four months old. Sandy thinks it will be a bit of a struggle with two of them to care for but she will probably provide care for the two days because her daughter doesn't feel confident with the other grandmother who is a worrier. Sandy does not like formal child care and neither does her daughter. She believes that children are better with their own family and with someone who loves them. She also believes:

> It's nice to have your own mother care for the child as they know better what to expect and are closer [to their daughter]. My daughter has a basic approach [to child rearing] that is similar to mine but of course there is a generational difference and they [the parents] are much more relaxed and less regimented than we were. My generation wanted to stick to a routine more, but it doesn't seem to do them any harm.

Sandy says that the limitations in the situation are that if there are things you are not happy with it is very difficult to speak up without hurting feelings. She also believes that it's more difficult for the paternal grandmother than for the maternal grandmother, as she is more fearful of intruding on her daughter-in-law's territory.

Sandy's husband, who is working full-time, has never helped out with minding his grandchild although she says 'he is a wonderful grandfather'. She also said that he didn't do much when they were bringing up their own children. At 57, he is still working very hard and not slowing down at all, and he is not confident in caring for children. In contrast, the grandchildren's own father is wonderful with the children, but a different generation has different attitudes.

Margaret and Bill

Margaret is now 66 years old and her husband Bill is 69. Margaret has provided child care for the eldest of her three grandchildren from when her mother first returned to work. Margaret loves being a grandmother and seeing 'the next generation coming on'. Their daughter and son-in-law lived with Margaret and Bill for six months from when their baby Rosie was three weeks old until they bought their own house. Living together like this meant that the grandparents had a lot to do with Rosie and knew her very well. Margaret said: 'We burped her, we changed her nappies, we fed her, we went through the teething, did the bathing—everything! It was very tiring at times.' Rosie is now five and will go to school next year.

Margaret and Bill also have a son. He and his wife have two preschool children, a boy and a girl, but their mother does not want to return to the workforce before they both go to school. Margaret and Bill babysit these two grandchildren and see a lot of them although they do not provide child care. But they have much more to do with Rosie because of the close bond between Margaret, her daughter, and Rosie the grand-daughter.

Rosie's mother had maternity leave until Rosie was nine months old and then she went back to work full time. When her daughter and son-in-law moved into their own home Margaret still looked after Rosie three days a week while her mother worked and she was in family day care the rest of the time. Margaret is at pains to explain that her daughter looks after Rosie too, and that she has not just been her responsibility as a grandmother. Nevertheless, the child care days are long and tiring, from just before eight in the morning until 9.30 p.m. because Rosie's parents usually come for dinner, and Rosie has her bath there and the grandparents read her stories and play games with her. Margaret and Bill and their daughter's family and son's family all live reasonably near by.

Now that Rosie is five she is in crèche four days a week and with her grand-parents for one day only, partly because she loves the crèche and being with other children, and partly because Margaret's health is not good. Margaret explains:

> I still thoroughly enjoy having her here and because we live close to both lots of grandchildren we are very lucky because we see all the grandchildren. The other two pop over quite frequently on the day that Rosie is here. The house looks like a tip after they go. They have a picnic and they do colouring in and then we play games like Snakes and Ladders, and Snap, and Thomas the Tank Engine.

Margaret says that Rosie thinks of both her parent's house and her grand-parents' house as home. She does not distinguish between the two as they are both home to her.

Bill has a slightly different perspective on the situation and sees Margaret as the indulgent grandmother and himself as having a more disciplinary and educational role with the grandchildren, but especially with Rosie because she is with them so much. He is now retired, although for a number of the child caring years he was working part time. He helps Margaret with some of the housework and shares in caring for Rosie. Despite seeing himself in the role of a disciplinarian he is a loving and indulgent grandfather who spends a lot of time playing with the grandchildren.

Angela

Angela is now 63 years old and has three children and two grandchildren. Both her grandchildren are girls and are the daughters of her two sons. She has provided child care part-time for both her grand-daughters although she also works part-time. The eldest grand-daughter is now 10 and the younger one is two-and-a-half. The circumstances of the two grand-daughters are very different. Angela says:

> Being a grandmother means a great deal to me. I consider myself very fortunate to have two grandchildren. I might never have known the older one if it had not been for her other grandmother. I have a lovely relationship with her — very special. Then there was the long gap — more than seven years — before the other one was born. She's lovely too, and I have a close relationship with her too, and I look after her every Monday.

The ten-year-old grand-daughter is the result of a brief encounter between Angela's son and the child's mother. Initially the mother did not want to have any contact with the father but her own mother said that was not the right thing to do and encouraged her daughter to allow the contact. The result is the child's father [Angela's son] and Angela as the grandmother have a lovely relationship with the girl who is now ten. The father sees her every weekend and Angela looked after her regularly from the time she was 18 months old. At that time her mother went away on a training camp for six weeks so the father and Angela shared the care of the grand-daughter. Angela comments:

> Over the years we have developed a very close relationship and I saw an awful lot of her in those early years. I took her to work with me at the office. The people at work got to know her very well and she was quite a character.

45

The maternal grandparents have their own special reasons for their concern that this grand-daughter should know both her parents. When they were only 17 and students at high school they had had a child and had been made to give the baby boy away for adoption. They married later and had two daughters but had not forgotten their son. These events made them very anxious that this grand-daughter should not suffer in the same way. Only recently they found and met their son.

Angela described how she now cares for the younger grand-daughter aged two-and-a-half:

> Her mother went back to work about a year ago. I look after her every Monday and Tuesday and every second Wednesday. She goes to family day care on Thursday and my sister cares for her every second Wednesday. My sister is unlikely to have any grandchildren for some time as she has a son who is only 22 and still a student. It does make me a bit tired after the day of caring. Yesterday we had a lovely day but a very busy day. I find that this son is not as good at the parenting as my older son. He himself was a 'terrible two'. My little grand-daughter refuses to go home with him; she wants to stay with Grandma, so I try to defuse this situation. I take her to the park and he meets us in the park and that works. We play a game that includes him. I get her at about 8.30 a.m. but because they live quite a long way from me I meet him where he works and he transfers her into my car. Then we go to the park or whatever. He picks her up between 5.30 p.m. and 5.45 p.m. and takes her home. It's a long day. It would be considered a long shift in a child care centre.

> As someone with professional expertise in child development I look at my son's parenting skills with quite a critical eye. I have given the younger son advice but I think that it is the mother that sets the tone, and she may have been brought up with stern discipline. Both parents are very keen on strict rules, such as you can't go outside without your shoes on. You must be clean! She has become quite defiant and there are power struggles.

Andrea and Robert

Andrea and Robert are in their mid-sixties and have two children and one grandson. Andrea is retired and Robert is working only part-time and approaching retirement. Their daughter Ruth and son-in-law have a close relationship with them and live not far away. The young parents also have a good relationship with the other set of grandparents although they live interstate and are not able to provide support on a regular basis. The young couple often stayed with Andrea and Robert after David, who is now 18 months old, was born by caesarean section. Ruth returned to work part-time three days a week when David was about nine months old, and Andrea has looked after him in his own home three days a week since then. Robert often helps, although he is still working, by caring for him from about 8 a.m. until Andrea arrives an hour or so later.

Andrea sees David as a blessing. She loves caring for him although it makes her very tired. She has always had a special love for babies and because of a serious health problem, had thought that she might never live to see a grandchild, so this has made him especially precious. She takes him to the park regularly, plays with him, and feels that they have a close and caring relationship and that he is very calm in her care. Her daughter is now trying to find some part-time child care in the formal child care system, partly because he is getting older and would benefit from the company of other children, and partly to take some of the responsibility away from her mother.

Research about grandparents providing child care

Australian researchers interested in experiences of caring for grandchildren found four categories of carers in a sample of grandparents of young children (although most were grandmothers) (Goodfellow & Laverty 2003). The four categories they found were:

1 *avid carers* who mostly lived their lives around their grandchildren

2 *flexible family carers* who give some priority to personal time while being very concerned with their family

3 *selective carers* who want to be defined more broadly, although grandchildren are an important part of their lives, and

4 *hesitant carers*, who did not anticipate caring for grandchildren and who recognised the need for balance in their lives and that they had multiple roles.

These researchers also found that grandparents who were from linguistically and culturally diverse families were more likely to be 'avid carers' with a strong commitment to passing on their culture and traditions to the youngest generation of their family.

Over the years researchers in Australia and in other countries have been concerned about the extent to which providing child care causes stress and health problems in grandparents; there have been a number of studies examining these issues. One of the early studies of grandmothers providing child care was undertaken by the YWCA in Adelaide (Binks c. 1990). Nearly two-thirds of the grandmothers in this study felt that parents preferred grandparent care to formal care and in many cases stated that they could not find suitable care or afford the costs. Nearly three-quarters of the grandmothers in the study did not feel that they were taken for granted by the parents of the children. Only a minority of grandmothers were suffering some stress and felt that minding grandchildren also imposed some financial strain.

A large and comprehensive study of child care in ten sites across the United States provides information on some of the positive aspects of grandparent care for grandchildren under twelve months of age (National Institute of Child Health and Human Development 1996). This study, because of its size, was able to compare care in many homes. It included not only grandparent care but father care and care by babysitters, compared with care in formal child care settings. This huge study took into account structural aspects of care such as group size, adult–child ratios and environmental factors as well as characteristics of the care-givers and observations of their care-giving behaviour. The researchers were concerned with aspects of care that were associated with sensitive, warm, responsive care of infants who were six months of age. They found that the closer that the care-giving was to a one-to-one relationship, the more likely the probability of responsive care-giving for infants. Where the care-givers had non-authoritarian beliefs about child rearing they were more likely to have positive interactions with the infants for whom they were caring. (Non-authoritarian care-givers believe in the basic goodness of children and that they learn actively. They do not emphasise obedience to authority.) Positive, responsive care-giving was more likely to be found in in-home care by grandparents, fathers and babysitters.

There is considerable recent scientific evidence about babies and their needs (Murray & Andrews 2001). It is known that babies communicate from birth and there is a growing body of evidence showing how crucial these early interactions are to children's development. We also know from research that one of the key elements of quality in child care is the quality of the relationship between the care-giver and child; closely related to this is an appropriate carer/child ratio so that the carer has the time to build a good relationship with each child. The focus on the ability of babies to communicate and to build relationships with care-givers supports the choice of one-to-one grandparent care for infants when both parents are in the workforce, so long as the care is loving and responsive rather than harsh and restrictive as supported by the findings from the study discussed above.

American research shows that a third of American children under the age of six receive up to 10 hours of care from their grandparents a week (Guzman c. 1998). Twenty per cent received between 31 and 40 hours a week of care, and 13 per cent received 41 hours or more of care a week. Grandparents in the United States take an enormous amount of responsibility for the care of young children because there is insufficient child care and the quality overall is much lower than that in Australia. Grandmothers provided more hours of care a week than grandfathers. A recent health study in the United States by researchers at the Harvard School of Public Health and Harvard Medical School has found that, after taking into account other factors, there is sometimes a downside to caring for grandchildren: grandmothers caring for grandchildren for more than nine hours a week have higher rates of heart disease than those who provided no child care (Lee 2004).

When grandparents care for grandchildren while parents work it means that there are financial benefits for the family and this is particularly important for low-income families. In the United Kingdom, where it is estimated that up to half of working parents rely on grandparent care, a survey found that grandparents spend on average about 40 days a year caring for their grandchildren (BBC News 2002). Rather than being paid for their time they were paid in kind by being taken out, or taken on holiday. Grandparent care in Britain has been estimated by researchers to save families more than one billion pounds a year and grandparents are seen increasingly as 'the glue that helps to bind a family together'.

Other studies in the United Kingdom of people in their fifties and sixties have revealed that the current pressure for older people, especially women, to stay in paid work may mean that in the future there are fewer grandparents available to provide child care for grandchildren and ageing parents or relatives. People between fifty and retirement are a 'pivot' or 'sandwich' generation combining work and care roles. Many have living parents and about a third also have grandchildren. One study found that nearly half of the respondents had a caring role either with an elderly relative or friend or with a grandchild and one in ten had both (Mooney, Statham & Simon 2002). Although both men and women were involved in providing care, the women's role was found to be more intensive. While grandparents were prepared to provide some child care, even at times to reducing their working hours, they generally did not want to provide full-time care, they did not want to give up their jobs, and most did not want to reduce their working hours. While many workers in this age group found satisfaction in their caring roles, almost half said that it made life more stressful, and in some cases, the health of carers had suffered through trying to cope with the strains of combining work with their caring roles. The cost of the caring was not for the most part financial, rather, it affected the carers' personal lives and both their health and their relationships. Australians in this age group are likely to be feeling similar pressures.

Grandparents from culturally and linguistically diverse backgrounds

Many culturally and linguistically diverse communities living in Australia provide considerable amounts of child care within their own families. For example, one of the many groups of immigrants who settled here after World War II are the Greeks. Many settled in Melbourne and it is known as the third-largest Greek city in the world. In my own street, in an inner suburb of Melbourne, there are a number of these older Greek families. I have observed the support provided by this older generation for their children when they had children of their own. I have seen the grandchildren dropped off and picked up from their grandparents' homes and have watched the grandchildren grow over the years. Unfortunately most of the older generation in these families speak only a little English, and I speak no Greek. Most of the grandchildren are now at school and some of the grandparents are now providing after-school-care and holiday care.

Some time ago, I interviewed Anthe, a second-generation mother from a Greek family, who had used grandparent care for her children. At the time of the interview, Anthe's children were in their late teens and long past the child care stage. She said that it is part of Greek cultural expectations that grandparents (although mostly grandmothers) assume that they will care for their grandchildren if both parents are working. In Anthe's experience child care centres are not well thought of and are 'not the proper way' to look after children. Anthe believed that grandmothers in the Greek community want to look after grandchildren because of the opportunity to spend time with them. The care is provided lovingly, and according to Anthe, it would be insulting to offer to pay for it. She used to thank her mother and mother-in-law by taking them out somewhere that they would enjoy. However, this is not the whole picture of the Greek community and their child care needs.

I met and interviewed the manager of a Greek child care centre in Melbourne and a Greek grandmother who, unlike Anthe, used formal child care for her children. These two interviews provide a broader picture of the experience of Greek parents.

According to the manager of the Greek child care centre, most of the parents who settled in Melbourne in the early days did not have access to an extended family and needed child care. Both parents usually worked long hours with the aim of buying a house. In the 1970s, of necessity, there was a lot of unregulated 'backyard child care'. In 1977, in response to this need, the Greek Welfare Society opened a bilingual child care centre in Richmond. The parents that used this centre in the early days are now grandparents, and because they used formal child care themselves, they have a positive attitude towards it, especially to this centre which caters for the Greek community. They want their grandchildren to come to child care partly because they believe that it prepares them for school, but also because they have their own lives to live. They want to go to their social clubs and to see their friends, and having their grandchildren at home hinders this. As a result the grandparents share the care of their grandchildren with the child care centre while still providing some care themselves.

Although many of the second generation of Greeks—the parents of the grandchildren—have moved away from Richmond, many of the first generation—the grandparents—still live in the area. A lot of the parents bring the grandchildren to child care on their way to work and the grandparents pick them up and take them home later in the day. The parents come to the grandparents' home to pick up the children and often have dinner with their parents, thus keeping the family close and cohesive. Other parents start work very early in the morning so they bring the grandchildren to the grandparents' home and the grandparents take them to child care. The parents then pick them up on the way home. There are, however, still some grandparents who want the grandchildren to themselves and discourage the use of child care by the parents.

The grandparents are concerned to keep the Greek culture alive, and like the Greek child care centre because it has a bilingual Greek program and maintains the language and culture. They communicate with their grand-children in Greek and take them to different celebrations in the community. The family structure in the Greek community is extended rather than nuclear, and there are always aunts, uncles, and cousins as well as grandparents at big family gatherings throughout the year. This keeps the culture alive and helps the third generation, who are more influenced by mainstream society, to have a strong sense of Greek identity and to keep up traditions. The following case study of a Greek grandmother illustrates the attitudes of some contemporary Greek grandmothers.

Maria

Maria, who is fifty, has three children, and two grandchildren aged four and two. Her son is still at home and attending university, and both her daughters are married to Greeks. The daughter with the two children does not work at present but Maria works full time. Maria says that before her daughters married she told them not to expect her to be one of those typical Greek grandmothers who drop everything and look after their children for them whenever they feel like it. She says she doesn't mind babysitting when it is something special like a wedding, but that because she works full time, the weekend is the only time she has to herself. Maria is pleased to be a grandmother but is also pleased to give the grandchildren back after looking after them.

The above discussion is about only one of the many culturally diverse communities in Australia. The following section discusses some of the research which has examined issues in grandparent child care in other communities. A limited number of communities are included, partly because not all communities have been researched, but also because the aim is to raise awareness through these examples of the issues in grandparent child care rather than to represent the full range of diversity.

Research on grandparents from culturally and linguistically diverse backgrounds providing child care

There have been a number of Australian studies of grandparents from various cultural groups who provide child care for their grandchildren. In general these studies have examined the extent of grandparent involvement in child care compared with grandparents from English speaking backgrounds, the time involved in child care, the reasons for providing child care, whether the caring creates isolation or satisfaction, and whether the rewards outweigh the costs. Sometimes the studies compare the experiences of grandparents from more recently arrived migrant groups with those of those who settled in Australia earlier.

A major study in 1995 was of grandparents in Italian, Vietnamese and Arabic-speaking communities (Lever 1995). This study aimed to develop a better understanding of grandparents' roles as carers, the relationship between the older generation and their families, and to identify ways of supporting grandparents from culturally and linguistically diverse communities as well as to estimate the savings to the community of this child care. Fifty-nine

Melbourne grandparents were selected to take part in this study. The group included 16 grandfathers, and was restricted to grandparents who were providing child care for at least two days a week. The groups represented people who arrived after World War ll—the Italians—and more recent arrivals—the Vietnamese and Arabic-speaking communities.

The study found that the extended family was very important to all people interviewed and had helped them to adapt to Australian society. Old people were seen as crucial and were valued in their role in maintaining cultural traditions and the language of their community. The importance of retaining the language and culture is one of the reasons the parents chose child care by grandparents rather than the formal child care system. These families also had differences in beliefs about child rearing compared with families who used the formal system of child care. They valued interdependence and mutual support rather than individuality and independence, which are the values encouraged in mainstream society and in the child care and preschool system. Family is seen as a priority and it is family that has assisted these migrant families to adapt to the changes required in the period of settlement in this country. However, some families from culturally and linguistically diverse backgrounds do also access child care and there have been great efforts made to make services accessible and supportive to children and families from all backgrounds.

The study found that the grandparents from these three groups—Italian, Arabic-speaking and Vietnamese—cared for more children under three years of age than for older children. But Arabic-speakers cared for roughly the same number of three- to five-year-olds and school-aged children as they did of children under three. Most grandparents cared for children from one family only in the grandparents' homes and most did not live in three-generational households. The grandparents indicated that the positive aspects of caring for grandchildren were passing on the language, saving money for their children, and the fact that the children were cared for by trusted family members. They also felt that they were being useful in the family.

Most of the grandparents in this study had few complaints, but the negative aspects of this method of child care which were identified by them were:

- getting tired and needing more time to themselves and with people the same age
- feeling obliged to provide child care when they would rather not, and
- finding the children hard to manage.

The most popular activities of the grandparents and grandchildren were shopping, watching TV, telling stories and playing games. Most of the grandparents, when asked their views of formal child care, believed that mothers should care for their own children but that grandparents were the best substitute if an alternative was necessary. Some grandparents thought that formal child care costs too much and some thought that it was acceptable if it was high quality.

Most grandparents indicated that they did not require additional support, but a few suggested a number of ways in which they could be supported in their role as care-givers, such as: additional help in school holidays, play groups, support groups for care-givers, help with housework, toy libraries, financial assistance and help with school work. None of the grandparents in this study received any payment for the care they provided.

The second major and more recent study of child care provided by grandparents in culturally and linguistically diverse communities is one which explored the health impacts of being a grandmother (Drysdale & Nilufer 2000). This project focused on the experiences of grandmothers in three cultural groups: Macedonian, Arabic-speaking, and mainland Chinese, which is a small but rapidly growing community. This study was concerned with the experiences and problems of grandmothers who were caring for grandchildren either full time or almost full time, and the effects on their health and wellbeing. The study also aimed to provide the grandmothers who participated in the study with information about community resources which could provide them with support, and to create community awareness of their needs.

Interviews were conducted in the participant's own language and took place in their homes. Thirty grandmothers took part, ten from each community. Ten of the grandmothers were under 60 years of age, and three were over 70. The grandmothers who took part in this study provided free child care for 48 children and it was estimated that '... the contribution of this small group to the nation's economy is equivalent to more than half a million dollars a year'. (This is a conservative estimate based on child care costs and the family rebate available in 2000.)

Fifty per cent of the grandmothers understood little or no spoken English and the majority of the mainland Chinese grandmothers were among this group. Sixty per cent of all the grandmothers could not read English. In general the grandmothers did not have the skills required to communicate with the wider community outside their family and cultural group. The Arabic-speaking grandmothers had never worked outside the home but almost all the Macedonian grandmothers had worked in factories doing process work. The majority of Chinese grandmothers had worked in professions such as teaching, and two had trade qualifications. Only two of the Chinese grandmothers had been process workers and none had been confined to their homes caring for their families. With the exception of the Arabic-speaking grandmothers, who had had large families, nearly all grandmothers in the other two groups had only two children; all had been married, although nine were now widowed. With the exception of the Chinese grandmothers who had no income, the others had income either from a pension or benefit, or from their husband's earnings. The Chinese grandmothers were the group which was experiencing the most change and contrast between their previous lives in their country of origin and their present lives. They had previously had a career outside the home and their own income, and were now without income or employment and were caring for grandchildren at home—a much more restricted life than their earlier circumstances.

All the grandparents in the study loved their grandchildren but only half said that this was why they provided child care. The most common reason for doing so was to help their children have a more secure financial future, so that they could buy a house and car, and generally to make their lives easier. They were also concerned with the stability of their children's families due to the pressures of work. Only the Arabic-speaking grandmothers mentioned the importance of their community traditions in relation to caring for their grandchildren.

More than half of the grandmothers had been providing child care for their grandchildren for more than two years. Half of them were looking after two or more grandchildren while others cared for only one. The Chinese grandmothers, who were mostly widows, lived in extended family households and had the longest hours of caring (more than ten hours each day) because their grandchildren were mostly under school age. Four of these grandmothers provided care 24 hours a day for grandchildren who were under two. The Arabic-speaking and Chinese grandmothers not only cared for and played with their grandchildren but also did household chores.

The Macedonian grandmothers cared for their grandchildren in their own homes and took full responsibility for them but did not do any housework other than their own. The Macedonian grandmothers reported no difficulties looking after grandchildren. In contrast, the Arabic and Chinese grandmothers reported problems such as tiredness, not having sufficient energy to participate in the community, not being able to afford their grandchildren's demands for treats and toys, isolation, not having time for themselves and not knowing what to do in an emergency (this especially applied to the Chinese grandmothers). They also reported differences with the parents over the care of the grandchildren including discipline and spoiling, and that these differences sometimes led to conflict with a son or daughter.

The Arabic and Macedonian grandmothers believed that there would be undesirable effects on their grandchildren's health and wellbeing if they no longer looked after their grandchildren. They were also concerned that their children and the grandchildren would have difficulty coping if they did not provide child care. The Chinese grandmothers thought that their children would have to work harder if they did not provide child care, but they thought that their own health and wellbeing would improve. The Chinese grandmothers had more positive attitudes to formal child care than the Macedonian and Arabic-speaking grandmothers. The Chinese grandmothers had experienced the greatest changes in their lives of the three groups because they had experienced not only loss of independence but also loss of income, and some no longer had their own home when they had moved from mainland China to Australia to care for their grandchildren.

Appreciation for the care provided by these groups of grandmothers was usually in kind and it sometimes included paying bills, buying food and paying expenses. In the case of three of the Chinese grandmothers there was some financial support as they had no income of their own.

It was pointed out in this study that the greatest benefit to most of these grandmothers was being a focal point in the family. This maintained their sense of connectedness within their family and was more important to many of them than other social contacts outside the family. Arthur Kornhaber, who founded the Grandparenting Foundation in the United States, and who was mentioned in Chapter 1, says that this sense of belonging and connectedness is in keeping with the findings of much research and is linked to self-esteem. He says that 'being an involved grandparent and family elder becomes a source of pride and gives meaning to life' (Kornhaber 1996, p. 153).

The Chinese grandmothers' experience was different from the other two groups of grandmothers for several reasons. One reason was that they were the newest settlers and still adjusting to the changes involved in living in a new country with different ways and a different language; another was because they cared for their grandchildren for longer hours; and also because they were more dependent financially in contrast to their former professional lives in China. Most of the Macedonian and Arabic-speaking grandmothers, on the other hand, had been at home or working in factories before retirement and had expectations that they would provide child care. The findings of a number of studies support the belief that there are also cultural norms that oblige grandmothers in some communities to provide child care for their grandchildren. The greatest support these grandmothers have in their child care roles is provided by grandfathers, where they are present, but this support is along traditional gender roles within the family and community.

Conclusions

While there are many satisfactions in grandparenting there can also be difficulties that are not of the grandparents' making. Family circumstances change over time and sometimes circumstances get more difficult particularly if parents are unable to care adequately for their children for one reason or another. Patricia's younger grand-daughter is at risk and has already come to the attention of child protection services because of the mental illness of both parents. So far the arrangements that have been made for her granddaughter's care have worked out, although the mental health of the child's mother is precarious.

Chapter 3 looks at the experiences of the growing group of grandparents who are bringing up their grandchildren because of their parents' neglect, illness or inadequacy.

References

Australian Bureau of Statistics 2002, *Child Care, Australia, Jun 2002*, Cat. no. 4402.0, ABS, Canberra, viewed 9 May 2006, (http://www.abs.gov.au/ausstats/abs@.nsf/productsbytitle/7D0F3D1C0AD1B230CA2568A90013933F?OpenDocument).

BBC News 2002, *Grandparents are a baby boon*, BBC News, 13 September 2002, viewed 6 April 2006, (http://news.bbc.co.uk/2/hi/business/2255156.stm).

Binks, P c. 1990, *Grandmothers providing child care in South Australia*, YWCA, Adelaide.

Drysdale, P & Nilufer, Y 2000, *'It's a long day on your own': exploring and addressing the health impacts of grandmothering in culturally and linguistically diverse communities*, Women's Health in the North and Victorian Cooperative on Children's Services for Ethnic Groups, Melbourne.

Goodfellow, J & Laverty, J 2003, 'Grandparents supporting working families: satisfaction and choice in provision of child care', *Family Matters*, no. 66, pp. 14–19.

Greenblat, E & Ochiltree, G 1993, *Use and choice of child care*, Australian Institute of Family Studies, Melbourne.

Guzman, L c. 1998, *The use of grandparents as child care providers*, Center for Demography and Ecology, University of Wisconsin-Madison.

Lee, S 2004, 'Caring for grandchildren increases women's heart disease risk', *Harvard University Gazette*, 4 December 2003, viewed 6 April 2006, (www.news.harvard.edu/gazette/2003/12.04/11-grandma.html).

Lever, R 1995, *Grandparents: the mainstay of modern families: a study of grandparenting within families from Italian, Vietnamese and Arabic speaking communities*, Australian Multicultural Foundation, Carlton.

Mooney, A & Statham, J, with Simon, A 2002, *The pivot generation: informal care and work after 50*, The Policy Press, London.

Murray, L & Andrews, L 2001, *Your social baby: understanding babies' communication from birth*, ACER Press, Melbourne.

National Institute of Child Health and Human Development, Early Child Care Research Network 1996, 'Characteristics of infant child care: factors contributing to positive caregiving', *Early Childhood Research Quarterly*, no. 11, pp. 269–306.

Phillips, J, Bernard, M & Chittenden, M 2002, *Juggling work and care: the experiences of working carers of older adults*, The Policy Press, London.

Chapter 3

Grandparents bringing up grandchildren

There have always been some grandparents who have brought up grandchildren. Sometimes it has been because a daughter has had a child outside of marriage, sometimes because of the death of the grandchild's parents, and sometimes because the parents are unable to care for the child themselves due to physical or mental illness, incapacity or abandonment. Grandparents are still bringing up grandchildren for these reasons, but what is new is the increase in the number of grandparents parenting grandchildren due to substance abuse, involving alcohol and/or drugs, by the parents or a parent of their grandchildren. Substance abuse has increased markedly over the last decade or so; for example, the number of heroin users in Australia almost doubled between 1995 and 2000. Because substance abuse involves individuals from across the social spectrum, grandparents from any strata of society may find it necessary to take over responsibility for their grandchildren. In the Aboriginal community there is an over-representation of substance abusers, including many parents, due to the cultural losses mentioned earlier.

Sylvie de Toledo, a young American woman, became aware of the issues facing grandparents bringing up grandchildren when she saw her parents take over responsibility for her un-partnered sister's eight-year-old son when her sister died suddenly. The difficulties her parents faced taking on this role later in life spurred Sylvie to work with other grandparents and to set up 'Grandparents as Parents' support groups in California. She briefly sums up the situation of these grandparents:

Some (grandparents) are as young as 35, others are in their 70s. Some are even great-grandparents and step-grandparents. They cross economic lines, social lines, and religious lines. They become care-givers because of abandonment, neglect, and abuse, as well as the death by illness, accident, suicide and murder. In some instances their adult children are in jail or mentally ill. By far, the most common reason grandparents raise grandchildren is parental drug and alcohol abuse (de Toledo & Brown 1995, p. 2).

This description could equally apply to Australian grandparents bringing up grandchildren.

Substance abuse by parents puts their children at risk. Children may be abused and/or neglected and do not have the usual developmental experiences of children in most families. Their parents are not only affected by the substances they are addicted to but are also likely to be in and out of jail and rehabilitation centres. Life for their children is a series of upheavals, uncertainty and sometimes turmoil. Some children of substance abusers, but particularly the children of heroin users, experience the death of one or both parents from drug overdoses. The number of deaths from heroin overdoses in Australia has been estimated to be the same as the national road toll, although not all these individuals have children.

The increasing numbers of grandparents rearing grandchildren is not unique to Australia. The United States and other Western countries are experiencing similar trends. According to the United States Census 2000 data, the number of children being brought up by grandparents has increased by 78 per cent over the last decade. In the American population, which is much larger than that of Australia, around 2.4 million grandparents have major responsibility for 4.5 million grandchildren. While there are no exact figures for the United Kingdom, the British Social Attitudes Survey (2001) suggests that there are about 100,000 children under 13 living with grandparents.

Until recently there were no exact figures available in Australia to show the number of grandparents rearing grandchildren, although it was known that the numbers were increasing. This omission has now been redressed by the Australian Bureau of Statistics and in 2004 data was released which provides an overview of Australian grandparent-headed families. There are 31,100 children aged up to 17 years of age who live in 22,500 grandparent-headed families. In Indigenous communities the proportion of grandparents bringing up grandchildren is higher than in the non-Indigenous population, mainly due to substance abuse by parents in the context of cultural loss.

There are also increases in the number of grandparents caring for grand-children in less developed countries. In African countries, and increasingly in Asia, a major reason for grandparent care is the death of the parents from AIDS-related illnesses, as AIDS is rife in the heterosexual population. In many of the poorer Asian countries grandparents in rural areas care for grandchildren while the parents go to the city for work or move to the Middle East, Hong Kong or Japan to earn a living doing domestic work or by providing other forms of cheap labour.

Reviews of issues about grandparents parenting grandchildren

In the early 1990s researchers, the media, and policy makers in the United States began to take an interest in the massive increases in grandparent-headed families. This led to congressional hearings at both State and Federal level which focused on the causes of the trend and issues relating to grandparents' access to public assistance. Three hearings which took place in the United States' House of Representatives and Senate between 1990 and 1992 looked specifically at grandparents' rights, their new roles and responsibilities, and issues of parenting a second generation. It was found that a large proportion of the grandchildren were the children of drug users and that these children also made up a large proportion of child protection clients. Recent data in the United States indicates that the number of grandparents raising grandchildren for these reasons continues to grow.

In Australia in 2003, the Federal Minister for Children and Youth Affairs, in response to the trends discussed above, commissioned a report on issues related to grandparents raising grandchildren. Grandparents were consulted widely about their experiences, the support they actually received, the support that they felt that they needed, the financial and legal issues involved, and any other relevant concerns that they had including health and parenting issues. Of the 499 grandparents who were consulted for the report, 72 per cent had to take on the responsibility as a result of maternal substance abuse.

The Australian report, *Grandparents Raising Grandchildren*, confirmed many of the same concerns that had been reported in the United States. The Western Australian State government also examined issues related to grandparents raising grandchildren and after finding similar concerns, have developed a range of resources to support them. Generally there is an increasing awareness, supported by the media and by various organisations, of the difficulties facing grandparents who are bringing up their grandchildren. A number of support groups for grandparents in this situation are now available in all states.

The Mirabel Foundation, which supports children who have been orphaned or abandoned due to parental drug abuse, points out the many difficulties faced by grandparents in these circumstances. It argues that the 'silent legacy' of drugs has led to:

> the emergence of a group of older adults who become surrogate parents because of the death, illness and impairment of parents from drug use. Vulnerable children enter the lives of older adults who themselves become vulnerable and need to be nurtured and supported as they face the challenge of parenting children in their senior years (Patton 2003, p. 6).

Of major concern is that these vulnerable grandparent-headed families are poorer than other families, and that the children have often suffered in many ways while living with their parents. Analysis of 1997 United States census data indicates that grandparent-headed families are more likely to be in poverty than other families, and this is especially so in grandmother-headed families where no partner is present. Almost two-thirds of children living in grandmother-only households were in poverty, compared with only 19 per cent of children living with both parents. Similarly, in Australia, it has been found that many children living with their grandparents are disadvantaged by the lack of financial resources. Two-thirds of Australian grandparent families live on a government pension or allowance. However the safety net of the Medicare health system in Australia provides better health care for these children than in the United States where many of the grandparents do not have health insurance because they are no longer employed. Health insurance in the US is usually provided as a component of employment benefits and there is very little support for the unemployed and even less for the working poor.

The transition to responsibility

Only occasionally do the events which bring about the change to full-time care of grandchildren come as a complete surprise. It may be different in the United States, where children frequently move away from their parents at quite a young age, so grandparents may be unaware of what their children are doing and what is happening to their grandchildren. In Australia, where there is less mobility, children are much more likely to maintain some contact with their parents, and the events leading to the grandparents taking responsibility for grandchildren are less likely to be totally unexpected.

The transition to full-time care and responsibility for grandchildren usually occurs over a period of time during which the grandparents become increasingly anxious and aware that all is not well in the family of their son or daughter. The exception is where there is a sudden death. The grandparents may already have been assisting the family in a variety of ways, including caring for the grandchildren on a regular basis, or whenever they think it is necessary, and they may also have provided some financial help. Sometimes grandparents may take the grandchildren into their care without the agreement of the parents, or child protection services or the police may have called on them to provide care in a crisis.

The following five case studies illustrate this. They are based on interviews with grandparents who are parenting their grandchildren. The names of family members have been changed for purposes of confidentiality. Three of these five grandparent families are the result of substance abuse by the parents of the grandchildren. In the other families the grandparents are bringing up their grandchildren for quite different reasons. In the first one, the parent of the grandchild has an intellectual disability. The second is the result of cultural and religious differences between the parents and some violence and threats. All these grandparent families have some similarities as well as differences, whether they are the result of substance abuse or came about for some other reason.

The case studies provide a down-to-earth description of the issues that the grandparents must contend with in their everyday life. Interviewing the grandparents was not only informative but it was a salutary experience for me personally. I already knew the issues involved from various reports, but that is not the same as hearing from people who are living with those problems every day. After each interview, where these busy grandparents gave up their limited and precious time, I arrived home very grateful for my peaceful house and my independence.

Three grandmothers are parenting grandchildren as a result of substance abuse. Judith's daughter is an alcoholic; Petra's son is drug-addicted, and Linda has two sons addicted to drugs. Petra and Linda are married; Judith is single.

Three major pathways have been found for grandchildren becoming the responsibility of their grandparents. These are: through informal arrangements made within the family, through State legislation relating to child protection, and through Commonwealth Family Law. These different pathways are not mutually exclusive, as children may be involved in all three at different times, as can be seen in the following case studies.

Judith (alcohol)

Judith, a librarian, has four adult children, and was in her late fifties at the time she took over care of two grandchildren. She had been aware that her youngest daughter and son-in-law were neglecting their two young grandchildren due to alcohol abuse and she was also aware that her son-in-law could be violent. She had visited most weekends to look after the children. However, the situation did not improve and the children, a boy of almost four, and a girl aged five years, were neglected.

Finally, Judith offered to have her grand-daughter during the week in order to send her to school but her daughter asked her to take her grandson as well. The plan was that the grandchildren would be picked up by their parents each weekend. However, the parents never came to pick up the children and they remained in Judith's full-time care. They are now aged 12 and 14. This informal arrangement made it difficult for Judith, but she did not take legal action to obtain custody for fear of upsetting the parents and causing trouble for the children. She received no financial support from the parents or from government sources. She found herself with the responsibility for both children but without any clear legal status. At the time the grandchildren came to her she was still working but soon had to stop work. She also had to sell her small two-bedroom house in an inner suburb and move to an outer suburb where she could afford a more suitable house which had space for children.

Petra and Bob (drugs)

Petra and her husband Bob are bringing up two grandchildren, a girl of 14 and a boy of 12. There was no sudden transition to grandparent care as the children had lived with their grandparents on and off all their lives. When the grandchildren were younger their drug-addicted parents also sometimes lived with the grandparents. Petra and Bob always took the children when the parents were in rehabilitation. From a very young age the older child learned to contact her grandparents when things were out of control at home. Petra said that finally, when she realised the grandchildren were really at risk, she had successfully applied to the Family Court for custody. Their mother was heartbroken over this, took a drug overdose and died.

Although Petra and her husband have custody of the two children, their father also stays on and off when he is not in jail or on a rehabilitation program. Petra says that it is very difficult when the father is living with them because '… it's another child in the house'.

Linda (drugs)

Linda (56) has two sons with drug problems and on occasion has had to care for up to six grandchildren. The first son was involved with drugs from when he was 18, and was only 19 when his first daughter was born. His partner was also involved in drugs and was 18 at the time of her daughter's birth. Linda helped out from the beginning to give the young couple a chance to get some sleep. At the time her son had a good job in sales, however he began to steal to support his habit and ended up in prison. The mother, who was also on drugs, went 'off the rails' and also ended up in prison. In the beginning Linda and her husband lent them money, bailed them out, fed them, and cared for the child while they were in rehabilitation. But years have passed since then and they no longer lend money or have the same expectations that their son will eventually be drug free.

Although the baby was neglected by her parents, Linda took over her care so there was no involvement with child protection services. The police became involved after the birth of the second child when the mother abandoned her in the hospital, and while the father was in prison. However, again Linda took the baby and applied for custody of both children through the Family Court. She has brought up both girls; the father is also in and out of her place when he is out of jail. He has spent a total of 14 years in prison, but keeps going back on drugs. Occasionally the mother has tried to care for the girls after periods in rehabilitation, but has never been able to continue for more than a few weeks. Linda continued to make sure that they got to kindergarten and school even when they were with their mother. There was also a longer period when they were in their mother's care while she was living in another town in the same house as Linda's first husband (who has a problem with violence). Once the son took the girls in with him when he got back together with their mother for a short period, but that ended in violence, and again they came back to their grandmother. The mother also had two sons over the years, one of whom is the child of another man, but the pattern of care has been very similar. Although Linda does not have legal custody of these boys, she has had to care for them at times.

The situation is similar but slightly different with her second son and his wife and children. In this case child protection services were involved after domestic violence. Linda was asked to care for these two boys. At the time she also had two boys from the first family as well as the two grand-daughters for whom she had custody. She was given a Carer's Allowance for having the boys, and the Department of Human Services Victoria helped her with housing. She feels that the Department has been very fair to her and they also have kept a check on the wellbeing of the boys.

These three grandparent families provide a picture of the transition to grandparent responsibility for grandchildren where substance abuse is involved. What is clear is that there is always upheaval and sometimes confusion for all involved and that the disturbance may be repeated at other times when the parents come to stay or when the parents take over care of the children for a time. Judith is the only grandparent who has had no direct interference from the parents of the grandchildren and has not had them stay within her household.

As explained in the introduction to this chapter, Aboriginal families have an even higher problem with substance abuse than the non-Aboriginal population due to the cultural losses they have experienced. Shirley is a grandmother in the Koori community who has successfully brought up three grandsons. An overview of her life encapsulates much that is typical in contemporary Aboriginal families.

Shirley

Shirley and two of her siblings were removed from their family at an early age and placed in a home. She said that the couple that ran the home were very kind and she has no memories of abuse, but she was separated from not only her parents but also her kinship group. She married and had five children—three girls and two boys. Fate was unkind to Shirley as both boys had intellectual disabilities and now as adults they live in sheltered accommodation.

Two of the girls started taking drugs very young; one was only eleven years old when she began. One girl died of an overdose but the other had three sons who were neglected. Shirley took over their care when they were very young and was able to obtain an order for their custody from the Family Court. However, the mother had them sometimes, and came to the attention of the child protection authorities who came to collect them. At the time this happened they were at the grandmother's house; when the child protection workers tried to take them away, not surprisingly she resisted, and finally showed them her custody order.

Shirley brought up her grandsons with financial and other support from Aboriginal agencies. She lived in an urban environment and experienced much gratuitous racial abuse from neighbours who realised that she was an Aboriginal woman. Life was extremely hard for Shirley when her husband died at a relatively young age. Other members of the family, but especially her third daughter, Beverly, helped with the care of the boys. All the grandsons are now grown up, employed and doing well, including one who is in the entertainment industry. However, Shirley still has trouble with her drug addicted daughter (their mother) who screams abuse at her for taking her children, and who breaks into her house and steals from her. Shirley has given up having anything to do with this daughter if she can avoid it.

Her health is bad. She and several of her siblings have diabetes and she also has bad arthritis. She is now living in public housing in a very pleasant new house and is to a degree content with her lot.

Other grandparent families

As mentioned earlier, there have always been some grandparents bringing up grandchildren for reasons other than substance abuse. The two following are examples of the transition to grandparent care in different circumstances. These grandparent families illustrate just two of the many reasons for grandparents taking over responsibility for grandchildren. The first grandparent family involves a mother (who was adopted) who is intellectually disabled from foetal alcohol syndrome, and her developmentally delayed daughter. The second grandparent family has problems of cultural and religious differences as well as violence and threats within the family of the grandchild. Again, both formal services and informal arrangements for care have been involved.

Alison and Nick (intellectual disability of the grandchild's mother)

Alison and Nick have a large family ranging in age from 44 to 18 years. Nick is 69 and Alison 64. Their income is from the aged pension and some part-time work that Nick occasionally gets from his previous employer. Between them they have three biological children and several adopted children. They have also fostered children who have needed temporary care. They are bringing up their developmentally delayed grand-daughter, Noeline, aged seven, who is the child of their adopted daughter Marcia, who also has an intellectual disability from foetal alcohol syndrome.

Marcia, the mother, had been living independently as a young adult, but went to live with Noeline's father's family. The father also has an intellectual disability. There was a period of turmoil when Noeline was a tiny baby which culminated with the baby's father throwing Marcia out of the house and abducting the baby. Alison and Nick, who were aware that things were not going well, received a hysterical phone call from Marcia telling them what had happened. The police rescued the baby and Marcia and the baby were taken to a 'safe house' run by a friend of Alison's. Marcia and baby Noeline then came to live with Alison and Nick. 'We went to court [the Family Court] and Marcia got baby Noeline on the condition that she lived with us.' This is a legally sanctioned situation and the father has access for a weekend every fortnight providing that the access is supervised by his sister because of his disability.

Jan (cultural and religious differences and violence)

Jan's daughter Heather met and married a Muslim post-graduate student from a Middle Eastern country while attending university. They had two children while living in Australia, and the father became an Australian citizen. The family then moved to a Middle East country where the father had a professional job with a good income; the third child was born there. The first inkling that Jan, the grandmother, had that all was not well was when the family came back to Australia for a visit. Her daughter Heather was pregnant with her fourth child. There was a fight between Heather and her husband. The eldest grand-daughter, Ayshe, said something that her father did not like and he dragged her out of bed and hit her very hard across the face. He later apologised to all concerned, including Jan. The family left Australia and returned to their home where the baby, the fourth girl, was born. Heather was ill after a difficult birth.

It had been planned that Heather would visit Australia when the baby was nine months old. The father arranged for Heather and the three younger children to visit his family in another Middle Eastern country on the way back to Australia so that his mother could see the baby. Jan was unable to contact Heather at this time and became worried as time went by without any phone call about arrangements for the visit. Finally she rang Ayshe, her eldest grand-daughter, who was at home with her father, to find out what was happening. Ayshe was very frightened but told her grandmother that her father wouldn't let her mother leave his family home where she was staying with his mother and brothers to learn to be a good wife. Finally after a number of phone calls Jan found out that Heather and the three youngest children were being held captive and could not get away.

Ayshe was very frightened about what was happening to her mother and sisters and became very sick. She was often left alone while her father travelled on business and was distressed about the separation from her mother. Finally, because of her illness, her father allowed her to come to Australia to have a holiday with her grandmother, but he would not hear of his wife leaving his home country and family. Ayshe arrived in Australia sick, emaciated, and with her hair falling out.

Jan decided that due to the circumstances she would try to keep her grand-daughter with her in Australia. After many difficult times, and with help from various people who knew more about the legal situation than she did, Jan was able to get a residency order for Ayshe. Jan has full medical rights for Ayshe and can make day-to-day decisions; there is a Federal police watch on Ayshe's passport so that she cannot be kidnapped and taken out of the country.

Heather was helped to escape and came to Australia to her mother's home for a short period. She was in very poor health and very stressed but had to return to where her three younger daughters were held because she couldn't leave them there without her.

Each of the case studies tells a different story of the transition of grandchildren to grandparent responsibility, but there are a number of aspects in common. This transition does not usually occur in calm circumstances. There is stress, worry and uncertainty involved and the transition stage is just the start of the story.

71

Issues involved in parenting grandchildren

A number of issues have been identified by grandparents parenting their grandchildren. There are financial and legal matters, issues to do with the children's behaviour and development, and changes in the grandparents' life-style and their own health. Each of these issues is discussed in the following section and, where appropriate, information from the case studies is used to illustrate the points.

Legal and financial problems

Reports on the situation of grandparent families in Australia and also in the United States have found that two of the major problems are the legal implications of taking responsibility for grandchildren, and the impact on the grandparent's financial situation. The complexity of the legal situation can be seen in each of the above grandparent families. The legal issues are not straightforward and are also closely linked to the financial situation of the families.

Reports and reviews in both the United States and Australia indicate that grandparents often feel that they are given the responsibility for the care of their grandchildren without the authority to exercise that care. Where they do not have formal custody of their grandchildren they may not have the authority to consent to medical treatment, enrol their grandchildren in school and so on. Grandparents may also have difficulty in obtaining Medicare cards for the grandchildren and are often given a range of conflicting advice.

Grandparents often find themselves in an unenviable financial situation when they take over responsibility for their grandchildren. Most grandparents have a limited income. Two-thirds of Australian grandparent families live on a government pension or allowance and in only a third of such families one or both grandparents are employed. Government pensions and benefits indicate a low level of income within the family; there is little to spare and these benefits are not designed for the support of growing children. Even where grandparents are in the workforce they often find that they are spending their own retirement savings on bringing up their grandchildren and/or in some cases on legal costs. This financial drain will make it impossible to do the things that they had planned in their retirement. To make matters even more difficult, it is not easy for grandparents to find out what government financial support they are entitled to when they take over responsibility for grandchildren.

The case studies illustrate quite clearly some of the difficulties faced by older grandparents on government pensions. For example, Judith took on the care of her two grandchildren, now aged 12 and 14. Her source of income is now the aged pension (although it was not when she was younger and first took over their care). She has found that the expenses involved in caring for her two grandchildren have increased as the children have grown older. Although she also receives Family Allowance from Centrelink she finds it impossible to survive without earning extra undeclared income from cleaning houses.

Sometimes grandchildren come into the care of their grandparents through the intervention of state child protection authorities when the grandchildren are seen to be at risk. This may lead to children being placed in out-of-home care with grandparents instead of in foster care. On application from appropriate statutory welfare authorities the Children's Court may legally sanction these services to work with the family. Legal responsibility for these children rests with the State, and grandparents like Linda (in the case of her second son's children) receive non-taxable, non-means-tested payments towards the cost of bringing up these children; she is also entitled to some tax relief. The amount of financial and other support varies from State to State in Australia.

If the grandchildren are under a Care and Protection order from State child protection authorities, these authorities have the right to the final say in regards to the care of the children. They may also arrange for one or both parents to take over care from the grandparents after periods of re-habilitation. Linda had this experience on a number of occasions when her sons or their partners tried a fresh start. Unfortunately for Linda's grandchildren, these attempts did not last long, and before long the parents were back on drugs and the children were returned to her care—a pattern that is not unusual. These changing family and parenting situations are very hard on the grandchildren and grandparents and can lead to disturbed behaviour and a lack of continuity in schooling.

At other times when child protection services become involved because of the abuse and/or neglect of grandchildren, they may ask grandparents to take the children as an emergency measure. However, when the emergency is over, because the children are safe with the grandparents, these services may then be withdrawn without any ongoing financial or other support being provided for the grandparents. In these circumstances the only way the grandparents can formalise the arrangement is by application to the Family Court to obtain a residence order; this was what Linda had to do with her two eldest grandchildren. However, there is no government allowance in these circumstances beyond the Family Allowance through Centrelink.

Grandparents may be reluctant to take legal action in the Family Court for custody of their grandchildren for several reasons. They may fear antagonising the parents, or they may find that they are not entitled to legal aid (usually because they own a house) and cannot afford the court costs. When Judith first undertook the care of her grandchildren she was afraid that her daughter and son-in-law might do something that would upset the situation if she took legal action or tried to get any financial support. She said: 'He [the father] is violent. He's still up there and still works in the same place. In the beginning he used to say he would help out financially, but he never did anything that he promised.' Some grandparents also fear being judged as unsuitable to care for their grandchildren.

The legal situation for some grandparents can be complicated, even where substance abuse is not involved, unless the parents are in a position to give approval of the grandparents' care. Sometimes the legal situation is very complicated, as in the case of Jan and her grand-daughter Ayshe, which is described above. Jan, who is 56, is still in the workforce, but the costs of the legal action she has had to take to do with her grand-daughter's situation have so far cost her about $24,000. Reaching this point was very involved because of the interplay of the laws of more than one country and the different cultural situation in each. For a while the situation was very tense, very frightening and very uncertain. Jan had planned to start working part-time and spending more time doing the things that she was interested in, but this is now not possible as she is supporting Ayshe.

Alison and Nick receive the aged pension and earn extra money when Nick gets occasional temporary work; it is this additional money which keeps them going. However, if there are additional costs it is difficult to make ends meet and the money that Nick has earned in the last five months is going towards their Family Court case for Marcia to take over unsupervised custody of Noeline so she can live independently (although still close to the grandparents). At present Marcia's care of Noeline, as indicated earlier, must be supervised by Nick and Alison. The father (also intellectually disabled) would like to take over full custody although he also has only supervised care every second weekend. So far Alison and Nick estimate that the custody battle has cost them about $20,000 for legal fees, as they are not entitled to legal aid. Legal aid in Australia is complicated because it is a State responsibility and each agency has different ways of functioning and making assessments of entitlements. This makes it difficult for grandparents to know what assistance they are entitled to in their State and their particular circumstances, so it is best not to make assumptions without checking the facts about eligibility.

Child development and behaviour management

The various reviews and reports on grandparents caring for grandchildren have pointed out there are often behavioural and developmental issues with the grandchildren where parental substance abuse is involved. Parental substance abuse is a known risk factor in child abuse and neglect. The children of substance-abusing parents have, along with their parents, usually lived a disordered and sometimes dangerous lifestyle. They may have been exposed to drug dealing, prostitution and other criminal activities. Some children may even have experienced the death of a parent through a drug overdose, as happened with Petra's grandchildren. At the very least, all of these children have experienced erratic parenting. In general, the children of substance-abusing parents are likely to have poorer physical, cognitive and psychosocial development than other children. Some are diagnosed with what appears to be attention deficit hyperactivity disorder (ADHD), but some of these children may actually have post-traumatic stress disorder which is directly related to the negative and disorganised experiences they have had with their substance-abusing parents.

The children of parents who abuse drugs and alcohol may have a number of special health and psychological needs including low self-esteem and feelings of abandonment. Judith's description of the neglect of her two grandchildren who were very young when she took over their care provides some indication of the difficulties these children have experienced:

Judith

> I sent my grand-daughter to school. That's why I actually had them because I knew her mother wouldn't get her to school. I said, 'Bring her down to me and I'll look after her during the week and she can go back to you at the weekend,' but they never came to get her. I said I'd take my grand-daughter but her mother said, 'What about her brother?' and I didn't really think that siblings should be separated anyway. I was still working then. After a lot of trouble I got him into a child care place, which was great, because he had had no experience. He'd never been anywhere with them; he'd been to the pub and the supermarket.

Drug and alcohol use in the prenatal period may also have negative effects on the physical, social and emotional health of children in both the short and long terms. Judith suspects—but cannot prove—that some of the difficulties that she has with her 12-year-old grandson, who has been diagnosed and treated for ADHD (attention deficit hyperactivity disorder), are due to his mother's drinking during his pregnancy, as well as to the neglect he experienced in his preschool years. His older sister does not have the same difficulties, but her mother did not drink during that pregnancy.

Where the welfare system and child protection has been involved in placing the children in the care of their grandparents, they are likely to be particularly vulnerable. If their parents are imprisoned, in particular, they may feel anger, embarrassment and guilt. There may be social stigma experienced by both the grandparents and the grandchildren because of the parent's actions. Although Petra's son has been in and out of jail because of crimes to do with his addiction they have avoided social stigma as far as possible by telling the grandchildren, 'You don't need to tell people that your father's in jail. Petra said, 'I have no qualms about that.' On the other hand, Linda does not mention social stigma, although she is distressed about the length of time her older son has been in jail over the years and the fact that he never entirely gives up his drug use.

Another difficulty for some grandparents is that children who have been neglected may not have learned many basic life skills that are taken for granted in other families. Some of the younger grandchildren may not be toilet trained at an appropriate age and may be unable to share or behave in socially appropriate ways. Some display aggressive behaviour, lie or even hoard food; these may have been survival techniques when they were living with their parents. Behavioural difficulties of various kinds are not uncommon in these grandchildren.

Children in grandparent care and the care of other family or relatives usually have more contact with their parents than children in foster care, although as can be seen in both Linda's and Petra's families this may be a mixed blessing for both the grandparents and the grandchildren. Where parents are present on and off in the grandparent's household (as in the case of parents who abuse drugs and even those who are mentally ill) the children may be confused over matters of authority, and may also have mixed feelings towards both their parents and their grandparents.

Linda does not think that the grandchildren she cares for have emotional problems but they have all had counselling. She says that they are accustomed to her because she has always been in their lives and they know her ways. However, she is still very upset that her eldest grand-daughter left because she was too strict with her. She regrets that she was so strict, but the girl will not come back and is living with a friend and her friend's father.

Children who are living with grandparents for reasons other than parental substance abuse are likely to have less difficulty but are also likely to experience some emotional problems. Children whose parents have died will naturally experience grief and go through a period of mourning. However, many other children in the care of their grandparents will also experience grief for the loss of their family although their parents are still alive but are unable to care for them. Where children have been abandoned by their parents they are likely not only to have feelings of loss but also of anger and fear. These emotions can result in behavioural difficulties or simply unhappiness. Very young children, because of their level of cognitive development, may believe that they are responsible for whatever has happened to their parents, and may need constant reassurance that they are not to blame.

Older children may feel that they are a burden on their grandparents. While they may be comforted by the presence of family members, they may also wish that they could live with their biological parents like other children. Jan's grand-daughter Ayshe (13) worries that she is a burden even though she feels safe with her grandmother and loves her. Ayshe misses her sisters, who are still with their mother in their father's home country; they cannot legally leave with their mother, and she worries about her mother. Ayshe has a counsellor who helps her with her fears and helps her deal with her anger towards her father.

A support worker who runs a grandparent group has found that some grandparents caring for grandchildren see it as an opportunity to make up for what they regard as their failings as parents. She has been amazed that grandparents, once they accept support, are willing to learn new skills. She says that they realise that today's adolescents are very different from their own children at the same age, and that they need to learn about the changes.

Grandparent lifestyle and roles

The lifestyle of grandparents parenting their grandchildren change no matter what the reasons are for taking on this role. Most people have expectations of their future regarding their work, their family and their age-related roles. When grandparents become stand-in parents for grandchildren it throws the expected pattern of their lives into disarray.

> In the expected pattern, one first becomes a parent and raises children. The children then form their own nuclear families, bearing and raising their own children. Grandparents remain free of parenting responsibilities in relation to grandchildren. That assumption is violated when the grandparent assumes a parenting role for a third generation (Jendrek 1993, p. 610).

Sylvie Toledo, who set up the Grandparents as Parents support groups in California that were mentioned earlier, describes the impact on grandparents' lives with feeling:

> At a time in their lives when they expected to be travelling, enjoying hobbies, and doing everything they put on hold while raising their first set of children, they find themselves back in the routine of bottles, diapers, and PTA meetings, sometimes 30 years after they last had kids in the house. Instead of doting grandparents who can spoil and coddle and send the kids back to Mom and Dad, they are surrogate parents with all the responsibilities of raising another set of children (Toledo & Brown 1995, p. 2).

Of course grandparents in this situation are often bringing up much older grandchildren and the issues may be different but the results are much the same for the grandparents. The children need someone to care for them and the grandparents fill the gap in a more loving way than placing children in foster care. Nevertheless, for the grandparents, taking on the role of substitute parent changes their lives in many ways and involves many activities more suited to the much younger parent generation.

The following issues of concern have been identified by grandparents with responsibility for bringing up grandchildren:

- They are usually not free to take part in the activities that their own age group are involved in.
- They may become isolated from their friends.
- They find that traditional support networks of friends and family may not be able to help out because they are not in similar situations and do not understand the situation.
- They are less able to enjoy and indulge grandchildren when they are responsible for parenting tasks including discipline.
- Their health may be affected by the additional work involved in caring for children, especially if they are older and/or already have ongoing health problems.
- They are always tired and often overworked.

Judith explained how the responsibility for bringing up her grandchildren had completely changed her life. She had had a serious health scare some time before taking over the care of her grandchildren and had reduced her working hours to half time so that she could do some of the things she wanted to rather than wait for a time that might never come.

Judith

I felt that I was in prison for a while. I had no life. My money wasn't my own. It just completely changed my life; all the plans I had for travel, doing things, courses, flexible working hours. I had subscription tickets to the opera, the symphony orchestra, theatre. I was never home. So that's just the way it is, there's nothing else you can do. I always thought that there's an answer to every problem. But I had to take them! Goodness knows what would've happened to them since if they had remained up there [with their parents]. I know I should accept it gracefully and deal with it but I still miss being able to do things. My four children were independent so early. At 16 or 17 they were off and doing their own things, and then to be hit with this just as I thought my life was free. I can't whinge about it because people don't understand, but sometimes I feel that my life has nothing to do with me.

Jan also says that her life has changed not only since she took over care of her grand-daughter but because of the frightening events in her daughter's life. She says: 'It's changed my life. My life was really settled.' She has ongoing fears for her daughter and her three other grand-daughters but she is powerless to do anything about the situation. Her everyday life has changed a great deal since having Ayshe live with her. Although Ayshe is 13, Jan cannot leave her alone as she is very fearful and insecure because of past events including threats of kidnapping. She also has the ongoing worry about Ayshe's mother and much younger sisters. Jan is conscious of the way her social life has changed. 'I think that I have to be very careful that I don't lose contact with my friends. The friends are doing different things and I am always saying I can't do that. I think that it will get better as she gets older.'

Grandparents who are bringing up grandchildren have little choice in their style of grandparenting because they are taking a parenting rather than a grandparenting role. None of the grandparents in the case studies are able to be indulgent fun-loving grandparents to their grandchildren, as they have too much responsibility. Nevertheless although Linda has enormous responsibilities for her grandchildren, she sees herself as a 'carer' and although life is difficult doesn't seem to have the same regrets. Linda would probably fall into the 'avid care-giver' category mentioned in the previous chapter, even if she had not had to take on the role of surrogate parent to her grandchildren. Her story is somewhat different from the other grandparents mentioned in the case studies. Linda is now only 55 years of age, as she married early at the age of 16. She had had all her children by the time she was 21 and has never had career ambitions, although she has had a number of jobs. Linda, who has other children and other grandchildren as well as the ones that she is bringing up, explained: 'I really think that God has put me on this earth to look after kids. I still do the usual grandparenting thing as well as care for the grandchildren living with me.'

Grandparent health and wellbeing

Grandparents report that their health is affected by the responsibility of bringing up their grandchildren. They must not only support the grandchildren through any emotional reactions but must cope with their own grief, anger, sorrow and sometimes shame. They may have very mixed feelings about raising their grandchildren: concern and affection for the children, but also resentment and anger at the parents, and at times feelings of frustration such as those Judith expressed above.

Most grandparents also have constant money worries and sometimes the distress and costs of legal action, as discussed earlier, both of which increase the stress in their lives. Many also have physical health problems, especially the older grandparents, and they worry about what will happen to the grandchildren when they die or become incapacitated. Out of the five families of grandparents interviewed for the case studies, three grandparents have had life-threatening major illnesses.

Isolation from friends in the same age group reduces their opportunities for relaxing activities that help reduce stress and provide enjoyment. Research in the United States indicates that caring for grandchildren is linked to depression and other declines in health, even after taking account of the effects of age (Minkler & Fuller-Thomson 1999). As mentioned in the previous chapter researchers have found that women who care for their grandchildren for more than nine hours a week have a much greater chance of developing heart disease than women who don't provide such care. The researchers suggest that these grandparents delay seeking help for their own health problems, have less time for themselves, get less sleep, less exercise and have to put up with more daily hassles. These things are even more likely to apply to grandparents who take on full responsibility for their grandchildren than to grandparents who are providing child care only.

Another study in the United States examined the health of grandparents who are raising grandchildren using a sample of grandparents from a national study (Caspar & Bryson 1998). Care-givers who were raising grandchildren were compared with grandparents who were not in this situation. They found that care-giving grandparents were significantly more likely to have restrictions on activities of daily living compared with non-care-giving grandparents, and that their satisfaction with their health was also significantly lower.

Some grandparents, particularly when substance abuse is involved, feel shame. They feel that they are different from other families and do not have a lot in common with other parents. Sometimes the parents blame their own parents (the grandparents) for their problems. This has happened to both Judith and Petra.

Judith

My daughter blames me for everything I've done, even though I went head over heels to help her. It's all my fault. It's the things I've done. It's completely out of kilter. I can't talk to her any more. We have the same conversations over and over: 'You did this,' and 'You did that,' and 'You're too judgmental,' and it goes on and on. I just said to her one day, 'I'm not talking to you any more. We've had this conversation so many times and it's getting neither of us anywhere. All it does is upset me for days.' I've hardly spoken to her in the last few years. It's really sad and I see all these other people who are supporting their daughters through drug problems, and I'm not doing anything. But I can't. I tried but I just couldn't do or say the right thing. All it was doing was upsetting me and it was taking my energy away from the children. So whenever she rang she just talked to the children and that was it.

Petra

In the families of drug addicts the issue of blame is big. He [her son] blames me and says things like, 'If you hadn't or had done such and such …' he wouldn't still be an addict. That is very common. So the relationship changes and sometimes the marriages of the parents of addicts break up. We have managed because we have always been friends but some do not survive.

A question that hangs above many of these grandparents is whether the grandchildren will become drug addicts too. Grandparents feel guilty that they have made some mistakes—as most parents do. With hindsight they believe that they could have done some things differently, although they did the best they could. However, it is important to look at the difference in outcomes for siblings of the child that ended up on drugs, and remember also that grown people have a choice about whether to continue their addiction or to take a different path.

Where grandparents have more than one child of their own they often have other grandchildren in addition to the grandchildren that live with them. It is difficult for them to take the same interest in their other grandchildren although the relationships are likely to be easier and more satisfying. As well as having other stresses, these grandparents usually lack time to spend with the other grandchildren and family members. On the other hand, sometimes the other children and their families are a source of support for the grandparents.

Grandparents' relationships with their own children

Over two-thirds of the children in grandparent families continue to see their natural parents, and this has its downside where substance abuse is involved. Most grandparents find that the relationship with their drug-affected children (the parents of the grandchildren) is a difficult one. These children (the parents) may resent the fact that their children are living with the grandparents, even though it has come about as a result of their own substance abuse. Sometimes the parents are abusive and upset everything that the grandparents have been trying to do for the grandchildren. Some grandparents have had to take out restraining orders to prevent the parent going to the grandparent's house. In these circumstances it is difficult for the grandparents to keep their relationship with their own children on an even keel.

A family support worker who has assisted a number of grandparents who have drug-affected children and who has facilitated a grandparent support group explains what sometimes happens to the grandparents:

> The parent will change their attitude and be nice and engaging with their own parents and so the grandparents let their guard down. They think that things are starting to get better, and they are starting to communicate. They let the parent of the children come into the house and then the parent will explode and abuse the grandparents, and the children are witnessing this behaviour again. The grandparents are working really hard to create a safe environment for the grandchildren but then their own children come in and blow it all to pieces. It's so easy for these parents to just wander in and out whenever they feel like it, to come and see the children when it suits them while the grandparents are taking all the responsibility. There are no rules for them. The grandparents will often allow them just to come and go.

Grandparents who are caring for grandchildren where drugs are not involved are not likely to have these problems, although they may have different concerns about their own children. For example, Jan is very concerned about her daughter who is unable to leave the Middle East country where she is living, because she now has legal custody of her three youngest daughters, but is not allowed to take them out of the country. This is an ongoing source of concern and stress for her and for her grand-daughter. Alison and Nick have responsibility for supervising Marcia in her parenting of their grand-daughter Noeline. Although Marcia has a small unit close by she is at their house most of the time, and they usually have to take her on holiday with them; they do not have a break from responsibility. They find it easier to take just their grand-daughter Noeline and look after her, as the continual presence of Marcia, who is 'a bit out of things with the oldies', is a strain. Other grandparents have other worries but they are less likely to have the conflict and the emotional 'roller coaster' in their relationships that is involved in substance abuse.

Concerns about the future

Grandparents who are parenting their grandchildren have many worries. They have worries about their own health and worries about the children. Where the parents are substance abusers they fear that the grandchildren may go the same way. Sometimes they fear that they will want to go back to their parents when they are older, even though it may not be a suitable environment for them. The case studies give some idea of how these worries affect grandparents.

Judith worries that her grandchildren may want to go back to their mother at some stage although she has separated from her husband and lives with another partner in a caravan park.

Judith

> They haven't heard from their father for about eight years. He doesn't keep in touch. He was violent. Their mother doesn't ring much—twice in the last six months. She doesn't see the children. She says it's my fault that I'm not friendly enough to her. She won't come down here. She feels everyone's criticising her, which they don't. She's still on the grog. Still living in a caravan park in a one-bedroom mobile home surrounded by people in a similar position. I feel half-angry and half-sorry for her because she's been like this so long now. I just feel that at this stage she should have done something. She had so many offers of help; everyone realised. I said that she could come and live with me and my mother, my sister, her brothers and sisters, but she just won't do it. She's still the same. I don't know what the children are going to think later on. How long does that bond last between parents and children?

Linda worries that her grandchildren will turn to drugs like their parents. The two grandsons who are the children of her second son have returned to live with him. Linda says that although he is working and shops, cooks and cleans for them he is not a good example for two boys aged 11 and 12. She knows that he still has a 'bong' or two at night and she fears that the boys will follow suit and become involved with drugs. She also worries about her eldest son's two girls of whom she has had custody for many years. The eldest went to live with her father (who is still on drugs) when she was 15 because she thought Linda was too strict. Her father got heavy-handed with her when he found her with a boy and she 'cleared out'. She was picked up again by child protection but would not come back to her grandmother's care. She is now living with a friend and her friend's father. She is attending school but she is also smoking dope and Linda fears the drug problems are starting all over again in the next generation.

Petra and her husband have always been financially secure but their situation is now very poor as Bob has been made redundant from his job. She says that they will have to go on the aged pension. Although she says that she is not worried about the situation because her parents were not well-off when she was young, it is a problem for her husband and the grandchildren. She plans to start a business to help the situation.

Alison and Nick are also pensioners but at present things are difficult financially as any extra money they can save is needed for the court case for Marcia to be able to have custody of Noeline without their daily supervision. They cannot afford to have a camping holiday this year. Alison says that in the circumstances it is hard being a grandparent but she still enjoys the other grandchildren. Her view is that, 'It's just lovely when each one is born. But I just hope they don't come to me!'

Conclusions

Grandparents bringing up grandchildren live with many unresolved issues and usually with ongoing worries, not only about the grandchildren, but also about their own children. They also have to deal with their own ambivalent feelings about the situation, the fact that there is little government financial support, and that it is difficult to find what little there is available. They cannot enjoy indulging their grandchildren, and they cannot simply hand them back to their parents when they have had enough. These grandparents are in many ways unsung heroes who receive little public recognition for their role and contribution to the wider community in addition to their own family.

References

Australian Bureau of Statistics 2004, *Family Characteristics, Australia, Jun 2003*, Cat. no. 4442.0, ABS, Canberra, viewed 9 May 2006, (http://www.abs.gov.au/ausstats/abs@.nsf/productsbytitle/E6A9286119FA0A85CA25699000255C89?OpenDocument).

Caspar, L & Bryson, B 1998, 'Co-resident grandparents and their grandchildren: grandparent maintained families', Population Division Working Paper No. 26, Population Division, US Bureau of the Census, Washington DC.

de Toledo, S & Brown, DE 1995, *Grandparents as parents: a survival guide for raising a second family*, Guilford Press, New York.

Dodson, M 2003, 'Nurturing tomorrow's Indigenous leaders', 2003 Family Oration, Relationships and Children Conference, Adelaide.

Fitzpatrick, M 2004, *Grandparents raising grandchildren, a report commissioned by Minister for Children and Youth Affairs*, Council of the Ageing, Melbourne.

Fitzpatrick, M & Reeve, P 2003, 'Grandparents raising grandchildren—a new class of disadvantaged Australians', *Family Matters*, no. 66, pp. 54–7.

Gruenert, S 2004, 'Nobody's clients: children with drug or alcohol dependent parents', Australian Institute of Family Studies, Seminar Series, June 2004.

Jendrek, M 1993, 'Grandparents who parent their grandchildren: effects on life-style', *Journal of Marriage and the Family*, vol. 55, pp. 609–21.

Minkler, M & Fuller-Thomson, E 1999, 'The health of grandparents raising grandchildren: results of a national study', *American Journal of Public Health*, vol. 88, no. 9.

Office for Seniors' Interests and Volunteering, (c2003), *Grandcare*, Government of Western Australia, viewed 8 March 2006, (http://www.community.wa.gov.au/Resources/Parenting/Grandcare.htm).

Patton, N 2003, *The effects of parental drug use—children in kinship care: a review of the literature*, The Mirabel Foundation, St Kilda, Vic.

Patton, N 2004, *Parental drug use—a recent phenomenon*, The Mirabel Foundation, St Kilda, Vic.

Tomison, A 2001, 'A history of child protection: back to the future?', *Family Matters*, no. 60, pp. 46–57.

Chapter 4

Grandchildren after divorce and remarriage

Separation and divorce are major disruptions in family life, particularly where children are involved; they are a source of great concern to grandparents who not only feel the pain of their own child but are usually also concerned about the effects on the grandchildren. After separation and/or divorce some grandparents may lose contact with their grandchildren or the contact can become tenuous.

In most Western countries the rate of divorce increased rapidly over the last two or three decades and many of these divorces involve children. Fifty per cent of divorces in Australia in 2003 involved a total of 49,000 children. While divorces are more likely to occur in the under-fifties population, older couples also divorce, sometimes as late as retirement age and this may involve grandparents. Divorce can occur in any generation of the family and is likely to be painful for all, but of greatest concern to grandparents in general is their contact with their grandchildren after the divorce of the parents. Matters relating to the divorce of the parent generation as they relate to contact with grandchildren, including legal issues, are discussed below. Issues related to grandparents who are themselves divorced will be discussed later in this chapter.

Relationships with their grandchildren after parents' separation and divorce

Discussion in the preceding chapters indicates the important roles that most grandparents have within the wider family network. The case studies also illustrate some of the personal meanings that grandparenting has for both grandmothers and grandfathers in many different circumstances. As a result of complex inter-generational relationships in families, the breakdown of a marriage in the parent generation affects not only the parents and grandchildren but also the grandparents, both maternal and paternal, and other members of the extended family. It is not simply a private event in the parent generation's nuclear family. British research indicates that grandparents are an important support for children when their parents separate as grandparents and friends have been found to be children's key confidants at the time of separation (Ferguson 2004a). Grandparents are also known to step in at times of family crisis such as separation and divorce and to provide support for grandchildren and parents.

Separation and divorce is extremely painful at first as family members, including grandparents on both sides, adjust to the changes involved. The separation and divorce of a son or daughter often means change in the amount of contact that grandparents have with their grandchildren and their own children. Some relationships become closer as the separated parents struggle to adjust to the new family circumstances and often seek the support of their own parents (the grandparents of their children). Other relationships, usually between in-law grandparents and the in-law child / parent, may cease entirely, at least in the short term, and sometimes permanently. Occasionally the contact with the in-law grandparents remains if the parent with residential care of the grandchildren wants assistance. For example, Patricia, who was interviewed in a case study for Chapter 2, continues to have regular contact with her son's children although he is separated from his wife. She knows that they will not reconcile and finds it hard that her son is blamed for the whole situation, not only by his wife but also by her family. Patricia has contact with the grandchildren at the weekends so she is not missing out on seeing them; rather, she finds that too much is expected of her as a single working woman. She feels that her daughter-in-law is not interested in being a full-time mother. On the other hand, she misses having coffee with her daughter-in-law, and their previous friendly relationship.

Divorce is not the only reason for discontinuities in the relationship between grandparents and grandchildren; it can also happen after the death of a parent. One paternal grandmother, who had provided child care for her two preschool grandchildren for several years, found that after her son's death her daughter-in-law made it very difficult for her to see her grandchildren. As a result the grandmother not only grieved for her son but also for her grandchildren. There had always been a poor relationship between the daughter-in-law and the grandmother, which had been mediated by the son's presence. When the daughter-in-law remarried the grandmother was very unhappy because she saw even greater barriers to her contact with the grandchildren. Sometimes grandparents lose contact with their grandchildren if their parents move far away and efforts are not made to keep in contact. Again, this is more likely if there is already a poor relationship between the parents and grandparents. However, the most common reason for loss of contact or reduced contact with grandchildren is divorce, and this is especially so for paternal grandparents when the mother has the grandchildren living with her.

Family relationships are likely to change again when the parents re-partner or remarry. Even when grandparents have had close contact with their grandchildren, the arrival of a new step-parent who is trying to forge their own relationship with the children may lead to a change in the amount of time spent with grandparents, depending on the circumstances. If the new partner wants more time with the parent without the children present, the grandparents are likely to see more of their grandchildren, but if the new partner is keen to develop a close relationship with the children and sees their relationship with grandparents as a threat, or is just plain jealous, the grandparents are likely to see less of their grandchildren. Remarriage or re-partnering sometimes includes children of the new partner. Stepfamilies create a whole new family dynamic with their own particular complexities.

The well-known crime writer Ruth Rendell, in her book *The Babes in the Wood*, describes how Chief Inspector Wexford, the main character in a number of her books, copes with and reflects upon the separation and divorce of one of his daughters. Wexford is fond of his son-in-law and is sad to see him go from the close family circle. On family occasions such as Christmas, he and his wife struggle when the new man in their daughter's life is present. They miss their son-in-law, who they felt really cared about his children. Wexford worries about his grandchildren as the new man tries inappropriately to show that he is 'good with children'. Wexford's personal reflections looking back on Christmas are gloomy: 'Grandparents—who would be one? You couldn't interfere, you couldn't even advise. You had to shut up and smile, pretend that everything that your daughters provided for their children was perfect parenting.' The experience of Chief Inspector Wexford and his wife is one among a number of scenarios from the perspective of grandparents.

Two important studies provide information about grandparents after the separation and/or divorce of the parents of their grandchildren. The first is an Australian study carried out by the Australian Institute of Family Studies. Information about contact that children had with grandparents was gathered from parents who had divorced several years before and who were part of a larger study of the effects of divorce. Each family in the study had two children aged around 13 and 15 years. The parents and children were involved in three different types of post-divorce living arrangements: resident fathers, resident mothers, and non-resident fathers. Parents reported that 80 per cent of children living with both resident and non-resident parents had contact with one set of grandparents at least weekly or monthly. The amount of contact and which set of grandparents they saw was governed largely by the living arrangements of the grandchildren. Children living with their mother were more likely to have regular contact with their maternal grandparents than with their paternal grandparents; the reverse was true if the children lived with their father. In other words, the residency arrangements of children have the greatest influence on which side of the extended family becomes more important in the lives of the grandchildren after the divorce of parents.

The non-resident parents (mostly fathers) were found to be the key to the amount of contact between their own parents and their children (the grandchildren). Frequency of contact was found to be influenced by whether or not the children saw their non-resident parent. Where a non-resident father no longer had contact with his children they rarely or never had contact with their paternal grandparents. Less than five per cent of children, in all residential and non-residential arrangements, rarely or never had contact with both sets of grandparents. Total loss of contact with grandparents is quite rare, although the amount of contact may be reduced in some cases, and the evidence suggests that contact with the paternal grandparents lessens over time. Thus some grandparents, usually paternal, may suffer from parental divorce more than maternal grandparents, but the degree to which this is distressing depends on the quality of the relationship and the frequency of contact with their grandchildren before the separation and divorce.

The following case study of a paternal grandmother who has lost contact with her grandchildren illustrates a number of the points made above but also demonstrates just how complex relationships in the extended family can be after the separation and divorce of parents.

Louise

Louise has two sons and four grandchildren—three girls and a boy—who are the children of her older son. The eldest girl is now 26 and the youngest girl is 14. Her son and his wife separated about 12 years ago. In the beginning Louise saw her grandchildren regularly, although she has always found her daughter-in-law to be a difficult woman. The children have always been troublesome and the grandmother thinks their mother has influenced them because she was quite bitter about the separation.

While the children were young they came to stay with their father for the weekend regularly, but as they reached the teenage years the older ones wanted to be with their friends and did not come so often. The father found it very difficult to make arrangements to see them, as they wouldn't turn up and would always have some excuse. Louise thinks that they also felt some disloyalty to their mother if they were too close to their father. The mother did not help the situation as she was inclined to let the children do whatever they liked, and there were problems if her son reprimanded them in any way. The mother has fallen out with her own family too, but Louise's son keeps in touch with both his parents-in-law and his sister-in-law. All believe that the mother has always been a difficult woman.

Things came to a head when the eldest daughter decided to move in with her father about 18 months ago. She settled in, although she didn't help much around the house, but she was very put out when her younger sister came to live there too. The two sisters fought violently, and on several occasions damaged the house and other property. Their father finally asked them both to leave. The girls took their time over leaving. After these events the father decided that he could not cope with his children any longer so he 'divorced' himself from them and moved house. He does not let any of the children know where he lives in order to preserve his own sanity, but they all have his work phone number.

Louise has found that it is impossible to get in touch with any of the children since her son broke contact. She finds it very hard when other women are talking about their grandchildren; she can do nothing but keep quiet about her own situation. She hopes that one day the children will come around, especially the second-youngest girl, with whom the father once had the closest and most compatible relationship. Louise says that, although she finds the situation very hard, it is much harder for her son.

The second major source of information on children's contact with grandchildren after divorce is the United Kingdom study *Grandparenting in Divorced Families*, which was completed in 2002 (Ferguson 2004b). This study, which took a qualitative and more in-depth approach, was concerned with the experience of three generations of 44 divorced families. Interviews were conducted with mothers, fathers, children, maternal grandparents and paternal grandparents, which explored many aspects of grandparenting in divorced families.

The researchers found that while there is much evidence of the positive effects of the warm and loving relationships that children have with grandparents, the actual relationships were sometimes not quite so straightforward. Contrary to expectations, it was found that most of the grandchildren did not want to discuss their parents' separation with their grandparents. The children were not turning to their grandparents to unburden themselves about what was happening in the family. Nevertheless, it is worth noting that other studies have shown that grandparents are confidants for children. The researchers also found that within families there was a 'norm of non-communication' where even those who had affectionate relationships did not talk about 'painful or sensitive family issues'. The researchers argue that this 'norm of non-communication' complements the norm of non-interference (discussed in Chapter 1) and relates to issues of obligation which exist in families.

Grandparenting behaviour in the families in this study fitted into four relationship patterns. These four patterns of grandparent behaviour throw some light on the relationships between the generations both before and after divorce:

1   *Grandparent as parent/grandparent as grandparent continuum*: Grandparents in this category had been very involved with their grandchildren before the marriage breakdown and often became substitute parents after the divorce. This created some difficulties for the grandparents as they often felt that the responsibility detracted from the fun and indulgence they had had in their earlier relationship with their grandchildren.

2   *Adult centred/child centred*: Grandparents in this continuum of behaviour saw their priority to be their adult child rather than their grandchildren, and sometimes ignored the grandchildren in order to give their attention to the parent. This did not please the grandchildren, who became bored and did not always want to see the grandparents.

3   *Partisan/ non-partisan*: Grandparents whose behaviour placed them at the partisan end of this continuum had strong emotions about the divorce of their child and negative feelings towards the former partner. These negative emotions usually did not lessen with time. Parents sometimes had to remind the partisan grandparents not to express their views in front of the grandchildren. Non-partisan grandparents either continued the ties of affection with the former partner of their child, or saw the

benefit in terms of continuing contact with their grandchildren, of remaining on good terms.

4   *Reluctant/enthusiastic grandparents*: This continuum emphasises the diversity of grandparents from those who wished to minimise their grandparenting role and were clear about saying 'no', to those who saw grandparenting as a significant role and an important part of their everyday lives. These attitudes pre-dated the breakdown of the parents' marriage. Some grandparents were not good with children, and this had always been so, and parents were sometimes disappointed with this attitude. Some parents felt that the grandparent/s could make more of an effort especially under the circumstances of the separation or divorce. Other grandparents were confident and enthusiastic about their grandparent role both before and after these events.

A minority of the grandparents in this study had been prevented from having any contact with their grandchildren after the disruption of the parents' divorce. This usually happened to paternal grandparents when their daughter-in-law actively blocked contact with the grandchildren. For example, one paternal grandmother had seen her grand-daughter almost every day before the separation and divorce and they had had an affectionate relationship. After the separation she no longer had any contact with her grand-daughter because her daughter-in-law would not allow it. It was not always the daughter-in-law who blocked contact between the paternal grandparents and the grandchildren; sometimes it was the father who quarrelled with his own parents and severed contact, or the father had severed contact with his children and that made it difficult for his own parents to keep up the contact with their grandchildren.

The researchers in this study contacted the Grandparents' Association in the United Kingdom. This organisation supports grandparents who have taken legal action to see their grandchildren after contact had been denied. Occasionally these grandparents had had a legal win but the grandparents often found that the parents ignored the court orders, with seeming impunity, and prevented the grandparents from making contact. As a result, grandparents who had lost contact with their grandchildren often did not attempt legal action as it did not seem worthwhile to add to the discord in the family. The researchers concluded that, where there are ongoing hostilities within the family, it might not be in the best interests of the grandchildren for grandparents to demand contact, legally or otherwise, as it could lead to increased stress.

Though the United Kingdom findings indicated that successful legal action did not necessarily result in successful contact with grandchildren, a small qualitative study of grandparents in Canada showed some rather different results (Atkinson 2004). Interviews were carried out with 12 grandparents (consisting of three couples and six single grandmothers, covering nine families in all) who had lost contact with their grandchildren, mostly through the separation and divorce of their parents. These grandparents were members of a Canadian grandparent support group, The Association to Reunite Grandparents and Families. In most of the families where the grandparents had lost contact with their grandchildren it had occurred around the time of separation, although in a couple of these families it was when a parent's new partner appeared. One case of loss of contact came after the death of a son. The other two cases involved drugs (discussed earlier in Chapter 3). All cases involved paternal grandparents whose sons did not have the children living with them.

Six of the grandparents took legal action through the courts to regain contact with their grandchildren. At the time of the interviews four grandparents had been successful and two cases were pending. In all four successful cases the grandparents actually regained contact with their grandchildren, unlike the grandparents in the United Kingdom. They found that despite initial tension between themselves and the adult child (usually their daughter-in-law), the arrangement settled into something that was very much like the previous relationship they had had, and they reported that friendly relations had been established with the ex-child-in-law. They said that cooperation improved with each meeting because, in the best interests of their grandchild, they had put aside hurt feelings and were flexible and used a positive approach to communication. These grandmothers were called on to babysit, to attend their grandchild's birthday parties and other events of importance, and sometimes the child even had an overnight or weekend stay with them.

What is of particular interest is the process the Canadian support group advised grandparents to take before approaching the courts. It suggested that they first try other avenues to resolve the situation before resorting to expensive and distressing legal action. The most highly recommended procedure is to write a sincere letter describing the effects of denied access on the grandparents and grandchildren. Seven of these grandparents wrote such letters and there were three successful resolutions of the situation without court action. Grandparents were also advised to try mediation through any agency possible including friends and other family members. Obviously this is not always successful, but as the results suggest, it is worth trying. However, it is also important to point out that the legal situation of grandparents in Canada is different from that in the UK—discussed below— and this may account for the difference in outcomes.

Research in the United States has found that a number of single mothers live with their own mothers in three-generation households after separation, but that this varied by ethnicity (Pryor 2003). It was also found that single mothers living with relatives had better health and were happier than those living alone as they usually had emotional support and help with child care. However, it could also mean interference with child rearing and stress on the parent–child relationship.

Children's views of grandparents after the separation of their parents

A study of families in the United Kingdom included the views of 467 children aged between five and 16 years (Dunn & Deater-Deckard 2001). The children were asked about their contact with grandparents and how close they felt to them. Children whose parents had separated and who now lived in either single-parent families or stepfamilies reported that their key confidants in the early period following the separation were friends and grandparents. Overall, contact was greater with maternal grandparents than with paternal grandparents for all children, not just those who had experienced the separation and divorce of their parents. The only exception to this was children living with their father and stepmother, who saw their maternal grandparents less frequently and their step-grandparents more frequently. Conversely, where children lived with their biological mother and a stepfather, there were lower rates of contact with their paternal grandparents. Stepfamily relationships are complex and the degree to which the relationships with grandparents are harmonious will depend on many factors, including the availability and closeness to both maternal and paternal grandparents, the attitudes of step-parents, and the ages of the children.

Where children were emotionally close to their maternal grandparents, they were on the whole better adjusted. It is interesting to note that the researchers found that the children's own reports of their relationship with their grandparents were different from their parent's reports about these same relationships.

Australian family law and contact with grandchildren

In the 1980s the issue of loss of contact with grandchildren after the divorce of parents led to the formation of lobby groups of grandparents who worked towards recognition of the role that grandparents play with their grandchildren. They tried to obtain changes in family law so that grandparents had a right of contact with their grandchildren after the divorce of the parents. These movements occurred not only in Australia but also in many countries including the United Kingdom, the United States and Canada.

More recently there has been recognition of the grandparents' roles in families in most developed countries including Australia, and there have been changes to the Australian *Family Law Act* which acknowledge the importance of the relationships between grandchildren and their grandparents. However, it is still not a straightforward path to regain contact with grandchildren once it has been broken off. The first priority after parents separate is to sort out their own arrangements for the care of their children, and the grandparents' contact with the grandchildren may or may not come into consideration.

Many parents sort out informal arrangements for the care of their children without court orders being involved. They often reach agreement about these arrangements with or without the help of mediation or counselling.

Arrangements reached informally are not legally binding and parents may change them as time goes by. Some parents prefer to make formal arrangements through a court with the help of a lawyer and/or mediator, and these arrangements are binding. Where parents cannot agree they can apply to the Family Court to make a decision and the Court will decide what is in the best interests of the children. The result is a Parenting Order, which sets out arrangements for the care of the children; this is also binding. Since March 2004, when new Family Law Rules came into effect, parents are required to try to resolve matters relating to the care of children through negotiation rather than litigation. Terms such as 'custody' and 'access' are no longer in use and were replaced by 'residence' and 'contact', which emphasise the right of the child to have contact with relatives as well as parents. However, the latest response is to use the term Parenting Order, which sounds more family-friendly.

In most families, contact with grandparents is worked out informally within the family without resort to the law, however where this does not occur, under the *Family Law Act* grandparents can apply for an order to see their grandchildren. The principle under which such a contact order is made is that it is in the best interests of the child. Until recently the *Family Law Act* has recognised that 'except when it would be contrary to a child's best interests, children have a right of contact, on a regular basis, with both their parents and with other people significant to their care, welfare and development'. Grandparents were considered 'other significant people' but were not specifically named. This is now in the process of being changed to specifically include 'grandparents' in the Act. This action has come about as the result of an inquiry into child custody arrangements by a House of Representatives Standing Committee on Family and Community Affairs of the Commonwealth government. This inquiry resulted in the report *Every Picture Tells a Story*, and one chapter of the final report is devoted to 'A child's contact with other persons' including grandparents.

A significant number of grandparents reported to the Standing Committee that the resident parent (usually the mother) denied them access to their grandchild/ren or that the contact was tenuous. Often there was no explanation for this denial of access or the resident parent claimed that the grandparents sided with the non-resident parent and tried to turn the child against the resident parent.

The Commonwealth Government, in response to the inquiry, has now released the Family Law Amendment Bill 2005, which aims to amend the *Family Law Act* of 1975. The change that is most significant to grandparents is in section 68F relating to the child's ongoing relationship with parents, grandparents and with other family members. The wording is to be changed to 'including any grandparent or other relative of the child'. However, the emphasis in decision-making about contact remains on being in 'the best interests of the child'.

Other proposed reforms to the family law system include a network of family relationship centres which will provide a single entry point into the family law system. These centres will provide information, advice and dispute resolution services to families to assist them in developing their parenting arrangements without the need for a court appearance. They will be the first port of call for families to access other services and to resolve problems outside the courts. The family relationship centres will be supported by a telephone helpline and a website. Grandparents will be able to contact these centres if they have difficulties with contacting their grandchildren after the separation and divorce of the child's parents. The government also intends to include information on grandparents' status in a wider education campaign on the *Family Law Act* to ensure that grandparents and other members of the extended family are considered by parents when developing their parenting plans.

Most grandparents who have had regular contact with their grandchildren prior to the separation and divorce of the parents would qualify as significant people in their grandchildren's lives. On the other hand, the grandparents' right to have contact with a child does not apply when it is not in the child's best interests, and this is what is paramount in this situation. The following is a checklist of factors which the court considers when making decisions regarding children's contact. It includes:

- the child's expressed wishes
- the nature of the relationship of the child with each of the child's parents and with the child's grandparents

- the likely effect of any changes in the child's circumstances including separation from either of the parents or any other child or person the child has been living with
- the practical difficulty and expense of a child having contact with a grandparent
- the capacity of each parent, or grandparent, to provide for the child's needs including emotional and intellectual needs
- the child's maturity, sex and background
- the need to protect the child from physical and psychological harm
- the attitude to the child and to the responsibilities of parenthood demonstrated by each of the child's parents or grandparents
- any family violence involving the child or member of the child's family (including the child witnessing family violence)
- the need to make an order that would be least likely to lead to further applications for parenting orders
- any other fact or circumstance that the Court thinks is relevant, such as the age and health of the grandparents, their physical and mental fitness
- the likely responsibilities the grandparents will have as de facto parents of the child
- their communication skills and their philosophy of life.
  (NSW Young Lawyers, Chapter 11: *Family Law Act* s. 68F (2)).

Grandparents' legal situation in relation to grandchildren in other countries

As mentioned above, there have been a number of lobby groups advocating for the recognition of the importance of grandparents in the lives of their grandchildren and particularly recognition in family law relating to divorce. These lobby groups have wanted grandparents mentioned in the law so that their status is recognised. Most states in America have laws which permit grandparents to petition for visitation rights to grandchildren after the divorce or death of a parent, although the court must decide if that contact is in the best interests of the child. Similarly, in Germany and Italy grandparents have rights to apply for contact provided it does not put at risk the welfare of the grandchildren.

In Canadian law access (contact) to children for third parties, including grandparents, is covered under the Federal Divorce Act and provincial (state) legislation, although only three provinces have legislation which presumes contact with grandparents is in the child's best interest. In other provinces grandparents may petition the courts for rights of access (contact) as interested third parties. The situation in England and Wales is different, and only a person with whom the child has lived for at least three years is automatically allowed to apply for a residence or contact order through the courts. Grandparents therefore must first seek the court's permission to apply for an order for contact with a grandchild, which adds a second step or barrier to the process. In contrast, Scotland is changing its legal framework to recognise, amongst other things, the grandparent's role in family law.

The 'best interests of the child', which is the paramount consideration in most legal decisions about whether grandparents should be awarded contact with grandchildren, is to some extent ambiguous and open to different legal interpretations. An analysis of decisions made in the United States relating to petitions for contact by grandparents found that the legal decisions revolved around three themes: parental rights, children's rights and child development issues. Parental rights rather than children's rights were protected in 50 per cent of these cases, compared with only 24 per cent of the cases reviewed where the grandparents were awarded visitation with their grandchild. The authors conclude that on the basis of their analysis:

> [P]arental rights continue to largely shape family law decisions and the meaning assigned to the best interests of the child standard. Children's rights are being strengthened by the enactment and litigation of grandparent visitation rights, but children's rights remain subservient to those of parents (Henderson 2005, p. 659).

Divorced grandparents and step-grandparents

As mentioned earlier, it is not only the parents of grandchildren who separate and divorce, but grandparents too. It is unclear how many grandparents are involved in divorce as there are no statistics available, but most people will know of some grandparents in these situations.

Some grandparents may have been divorced and remarried or re-partnered before the grandchildren were born; others may have separated and divorced during the life of the grandchildren and this may have a more direct effect on their relationship with their children and the regularity of their contact with grandchildren. When grandparents remarry or re-partner, step-grandparents are added to the extended family circle.

I am particularly interested in the topic of step-grandparenting as I was a step-grand-daughter as a child. My grandmother, who I loved dearly and with whom I used to stay for long periods, died when I was five. I remember well the warm feelings I had for her and how she told the story of the Three Little Pigs better than anyone else. My grandfather married Nellie, a single older woman who became my step-grandmother. I never thought of Nellie as a grandmother, as my relationship with her was quite different from the one I had with my grandmother. Nellie was a great cook and a very straightforward person, but she was not warm and loving in the way that my grandmother had been. I often stayed with her and my grandfather in the country for quite long periods in the school holidays. I enjoyed staying there and eating all the good things that Nellie cooked. My mother and my uncles actively disliked Nellie and I was aware of this, but it did not alter my feelings towards her. My grandfather was a very difficult man and after some years together, she left him, so my stays in the country with them stopped about the time that I started secondary school. I look back favourably on my relationship with Nellie, although it was not close; and I have always wondered what happened to her after she left, but she was a taboo subject with my mother and my uncles.

There is very little research on grandparent and grandchild relationships after the divorce of grandparents partly because there are so many variables involved. However, a study in the United States sheds some light on the topic.

This study, from the Iowa Youth and Families Project, collected data on 538 grandparent–grandchild relationships, including 45 divorced grandparents (King 2003). The researcher argues that from a life course perspective the disruption of divorce has repercussions throughout the family, with parents as well as grandchildren, and also with other family members. Analysis indicated that grandparents—but especially grandfathers—who have experienced divorce did not have as much contact or take part in as many shared activities with their grandchildren as grandparents in intact marriages. This may be due in part to the fact that grandparents who are divorced—but particularly grandfathers in this situation—tended to live further away from their grandchildren. Divorced grandfathers also tended to have weaker ties to their adult children and this is likely to be a factor in their relationships with their grandchildren, as the adult generation mediates contact between grandparents and grandchildren. Overall, the negative effects of divorce were stronger for grandfathers and paternal grandparents than for grandmothers and maternal grandparents.

Not all step-grandparents are as transient as Nellie was in my life. Some are long-standing figures and the family may regroup in ways that overcome the negative affects of marital disruption. A recent article in the *New York Times* (20 March 2005) discusses the issue of the divorce and remarriage of the grandparent generation. It tells the story of Blake, aged nine, who had eight grandparents attend his basketball game to cheer him on. Four of these were step-grandparents, and Blake, who had not been born when both sets of his grandparents separated and divorced, accepts them all as grandparents. Blake is just one example of the multiplication of family members that can occur if grandparents are divorced. Nevertheless, Blake's grandparents and step-grandparents had to overcome some early discomfort in each other's presence in order to share in the pleasures of special occasions with Blake.

Grandchildren in some families where the grandparent generation has experienced divorce have the power to bring the once-hostile grandparents together when they meet up at family occasions such as the birth of a baby, baptisms and grandchildren's birthdays. Such occasions provide a reason for getting over former estrangements, as the four sets of grandparents did in Blake's family. Of course there may have been some soul-searching before the first get-together, but these grandparents realised that they needed to rethink their attitudes if they were to fully participate in the lives of grandchildren. Of course this does not happen in all families and the hostilities, estrangements and heartaches associated with divorce and remarriage may continue.

Step-parents who have had a difficult time with their stepchildren in their own marriages to partners who had children from a previous marriage may find that becoming a step-grandparent to the children of their stepchildren is much easier, as the grandchildren are likely to accept them without hostility. Others find some unexpected hurdles. Anne, who had lived in a stepfamily for many years, was one of these. Her stepfamily situation blended 'his' children, 'her' children and 'their' children, but it was the birth of Anne's first grandchild, to a stepson, that was her first hurdle as a grandmother. She found it was especially difficult attending the first family function after the birth of this grandchild. Instead of being delighted, she found that she could not hold the baby, and felt grief that it wasn't her own biological grandchild. What added to her discomfort was the fact that she had to face her husband's ex-wife, who was the biological and 'legitimate' (Anne's word) grandmother of the grandchild. This meeting took her back to earlier experiences as a stepmother, and the feelings of awkwardness she felt in sharing the parenting of her stepsons with her husband's ex-wife. She felt then, and still feels now, like an impostor when the family is all together.

In contrast, Anne's husband feels quite comfortable in his grandfather role whether with his own children's children or the children of his stepchildren. Since the birth of Anne's own son's child—her own biological grandchild— she now feels much more like a legitimate grandmother. She has also found that it is easier to be a step-grandmother to the children of her daughter's partner from his first marriage, where there are no strong bonds, and she thinks that perhaps it is the absence of a past history that makes it easier for her to include them in family occasions.

Beth, who was interviewed in a case study for Chapter 2, is technically a step-grandmother, but she doesn't think of herself this way. With the three grandchildren who live close by, and who are the children of her husband's daughter, there has never been a problem; they accept Beth and David as grandparents without query. David and Beth also have grandchildren who live overseas and these children have more contact with their biological grandmother (David's former wife) and her partner (who is a step-grandfather). Beth explained how on their last visit, one of these step-grandchildren (aged 8) said: 'You're a fake grandmother; you're not a real grandmother!' Beth realised that this girl was trying to understand what it is all about:

> They've got three sets of grandparents and she was seeing them all within a month of each other. At first I was a little hurt, and then I realised that her step-grandfather, who is her absolutely favourite, is characterised in the same way as not a 'real grandparent'. But normally we're just 'the grandparents'. It has never been an issue. I can't imagine that if my own daughter has a child that I'll feel any different about a natural grandchild.

Rachel, a grandparent who was interviewed expressly for this chapter, has had a rather different experience from both Beth and Anne. She became a step-grandparent three years ago when her daughter began living with a man who had two sons. The boys are now aged nine and 11 years. For Rachel these step-grandsons were her first grandchildren, but another daughter and her husband now have a daughter who is 14 months old and who spends a lot of time with her. Rachel feels much closer to her grand-daughter.

Rachel and her husband have always tried to do their best for their step-grandsons who are with their father every second weekend and one weeknight each week. Rachel and her husband think that they are 'nice boys' but not really easy to manage because they fight a lot and are nasty to each other. Over the three years that they have been part of the family, Rachel and her husband have tried to give their daughter and her new partner a break by having the boys to stay from time to time. Rachel says:

> We probably see them less now that we have a grandchild of our own, but we see them at least once a month. We look after them and when they come over we do things with them. We take them out to a playground or something just to give their parents a bit of a break. We give them birthday presents and invite them to anything that's happening. At Christmas they

come and join in. I don't feel the same way about them as I do with my own grandchild. If I never saw them again I wouldn't be that pained. But I like them; they're quite nice; but I do find looking after them a chore. It takes time when I don't have a lot of time. I try to be inclusive of them and to show an interest in what there are doing. If they've done well at school we ring them up and congratulate them or go and see them perform. I don't think that I'm a very good step-grandparent with them the way I would recommend other people to be. I work very long hours and we spend at least 10 hours a week with our own grand-daughter.

Rachel is reflective about the reasons for the difference between her feelings for the boys compared with her grand-daughter:

An external person would say that we do all the right things and I think that we do, but the emotional thing isn't quite there. We fight over who is going to get our grand-daughter when she comes over, but we don't do that with the boys. But I don't think it's a biological thing. I think it's because they had already developed a way of operating before we came into the picture, and they haven't learned about our rules. They do have different behaviour patterns. With your own grandchildren, even if their parents have different ways, they know that in this house this is how you behave. Our grand-daughter will know this. However, the boys really like us and they like my husband particularly, and he does things with them, although he is amazingly strict with them. We play lots of games with them, that their parents don't do; we play Monopoly and so on, and do lots of outdoors things.

You can see that there are many different ways of step-grandparenting. Some step-grandparents may be close to grandchildren if they are known from birth, while others are less close and affectionate if the children are older when they get to know one another. However, step-grandparents can still be fair and make their step-grandchildren welcome and feel included without having the same relationship that they have with other biological grandchildren. There is not a great deal written about step-grandparenting and some of what is written is not particularly useful. For example, exhorting grandparents to 'love' their step-grandchildren is not very useful when they do not feel a great deal of affection for them. Nevertheless, step-grandparents can still have a good relationship with their step-grandchildren and get on well with them without 'love'. Nellie and I did not 'love' each other but we enjoyed each other's company. Friendship, respect, attention, inclusion and fairness seem to me much more important and achievable elements of relationships with step-grandchildren than the pretence of affection and love.

References

Atkinson, J 2004, 'Grandparents' access to their grandchildren: a contemporary issue', Research paper submitted for course requirements, Ontario, Canada.

Australian Bureau of Statistics 2004, *Divorces, Australia, 2004*, Cat. no. 3307.0.55.001, ABS, viewed 9 May 2006, (http://www.abs.gov.au/ausstats/abs@.nsf/productsbytitle/F356DBB7EA7A96EECA256F10007B6B1A?OpenDocument).

Australian Bureau of Statistics 2006, 'Population: marriages, divorces and de facto relationships', *Year Book Australia*, Cat. no. 1301.0, ABS, viewed 9 May 2006, (http://www.abs.gov.au/ausstats/abs@.nsf/Latestproducts/C0771D0225B882D2CA2570DE0006B864?opendocument).

Australian Government 2005, *A new family law system: government response to 'Every Picture Tells a Story'*, Parliament of Australia, viewed 26 April 2006, (www.aph.gov.au/house/committee/fca/childcustody/govtresponse.pdf).

Bainham, A, Lindley, B, Richards, M & Trinder, L 2003, *Children and their families: contact, rights and welfare*, Hart, Oxford.

Dunn, J & Deater-Deckard, K 2001, *Children's Views of Their Changing Families*, Joseph Rowntree Foundation, York.

Australia, Parliament 2005, *Family Law Amendment (Shared Parental Responsibility) Bill 2005* (Exposure draft 23/6/05), Canberra.

Ferguson, N 2004a 'Children's contact with grandparents after divorce', *Family Matters*, no. 67, pp. 36–41.

Ferguson, N 2004b, *Grandparenting in divorced families*, The Policy Press, Bristol.

Harmon, A 2005, 'Ask them (all 8 of them) about their grandson', *New York Times National*, Sunday March 20.

Henderson, T 2005, 'Grandparent visitation rights: justices' interpretation of the best interests of the child standard', *Journal of Family Issues*, vol. 26, no. 5, pp. 638–64.

Hetherington, J 2003, 'Caught in the crossfire: grandparents' contact after separation', Paper presented at the Australian Institute of Family Studies Conference, February 2003.

House of Representatives Standing Committee on Family and Community Affairs 2003, *Every picture tells a story: report on the inquiry into child custody arrangements in the event of family separation*, Commonwealth Government, Canberra.

King, V 2003, 'The legacy of grandparents' divorce: consequences for ties between grandparents and grandchildren', *Journal of Marriage and Family*, vol. 65, no. 1, pp. 170–83.

Legal Aid Commission, New South Wales 2005, *Family Law—frequently asked questions*, (Available at www.legalaid.nsw.gov.au).

Pryor, J 2003, 'Children's contact with relatives' in A Bainham, B Lindley & M Richards (eds), *Children and their families: contact rights and welfare*, Hart Publishing, Oxford.

Weston, R 1992, 'Families after marriage breakdown', *Family Matters*, no. 32, pp. 41–5.

Chapter 5

Diversity and challenge

There are some events where grandparents, at least initially, may be concerned but which are part of the diverse experiences of an increasing number of families. Two testing situations that are discussed in this chapter are grandchildren being brought up in a gay or lesbian family and grandchildren who have disabilities. Both of these circumstances represent challenges to predictable family expectations for the next generation. The third, which is both challenging and an exceedingly distressing situation, is the death of a grandchild. Each of these situations is discussed below to offer grandparents some information about the issues involved and to help, as far as possible, to reduce unnecessary fears and confusion.

Lesbian and gay families

Some grandparents may have grandchildren who live with lesbian or gay parents. As grandparents they may have worries about how this will affect their grandchildren, even where they have accepted their own child's sexual orientation. Some grandparents may have difficulty with the whole idea of same-sex partners, and especially same-sex partners bringing up children. Even parents/grandparents who are accepting and supportive may have some misgivings simply because they have had no previous experience of such families.

Over recent years, as families have become more diverse, lesbian and gay parents have become not only more common but more open about their lifestyles. They are also increasingly in the news, especially when the use of IVF for lesbians who want to be mothers is discussed. Because lesbians, both single and in couples, are more likely to have children living with them than are gay men, the focus in this section is largely on lesbian families. However, the issues for grandparents are essentially the same.

The 1996 Australian Census indicated that there were 8296 female same-sex couples and that 1483 of these were couples with children. There were also 11,288 same-sex male couples but only 275 of these had children living with them. These figures are likely to be an under-representation of the number of children being brought up by lesbians and gays, as non-cohabiting couples and single lesbians were not included. The majority of children of lesbian mothers and gay fathers were conceived in heterosexual relationships but there are indications among lesbians of an increasing wish to have children. Two studies of lesbians in New South Wales found that in 1995 about 20 per cent of lesbians in the sample already had children and about 15 per cent wanted to have children; by 1999 these percentages had increased to 22 per cent who already had children and 20 per cent who wanted to have children in the next five years.

Although homosexuality is accepted and no longer hidden, it is still an emotionally charged topic for many and there is still some prejudice. Parents these days are much more likely to accept the fact that their son or daughter is gay or lesbian than in the past, but it is still frequently a shock when they 'come out'. It often takes parents some time to become accustomed to the fact that their son or daughter is lesbian or gay. They may go through a grieving process as they adjust to the idea of a future different from the typical expectations that most parents have for their children of a conventional marriage and children, before they reach full acceptance. Older generations are less used to openly gay and lesbian families and I certainly knew of none when I was a young mother. Organisations such as Parents and Friends of Lesbians and Gays (PFLAG) assist parents to work through their feelings and any issues when their children 'come out' and help them to take a supportive and accepting attitude. It is just one step further on this journey for grandparents to come to terms with having grandchildren living in a lesbian or gay relationship.

It is a relatively new situation for grandchildren to have openly gay or lesbian parents, and there are not many precedents for grandparents. They may or may not already have grandchildren who are the children of 'straight' heterosexual children and may wonder what their role will be when the parent generation is the same sex. The following interview with Linda, a mother whose daughter is expecting a child in a lesbian relationship, raises some of the issues involved. Linda already has a grand-daughter whose parents are heterosexual, and although she has completely accepted and approves of her second daughter's relationship with a woman she has some concerns about the baby. These are her thoughts:

Linda

I am absolutely delighted that my daughter has gone through IVF and is pregnant. She's worried, particularly since she knows that she is having a boy, that we won't be as thrilled with her baby as we are with her sister's baby girl. She says that we like girls best. I have concerns for the child because it is a boy in a lesbian relationship, but I feel really delighted because we really like her partner. She's just lovely and she is in the IVF program too. So that means that we are going to have two grandchildren in that family.

You have to tread carefully. I couldn't actually say [to them], 'What's this child going to call you? Is it going to be Mummy One and Mummy Two?' How are they going to handle it? You have to wait until they tell you because it's an unknown field and there's no normative behaviour for that.

My daughter asked how I will view her partner's baby when she gets pregnant, and I said that I believe that they are equal parents to both children. She said, 'Does that mean that we are both mothers?' I said that I don't know how you want to define your roles but whatever they are, they're equal. They both also asked me what my role would be, and I said that I would be an equal grandmother to both of them, and that the babies would be siblings.

The partner's mother has said that of course my daughter's baby won't be really her grandchild so he won't be able to call her Nanna. The partner told her mother that whatever you tell the first baby to call you is what my baby is going to call you, so you had better choose carefully. I feel that I have passed this test.

One issue for me is will the partner, as a biological mother, let me see her baby as much as my daughter will? I don't want to be cut out. These are unknown things in a way. I have a really good relationship with both of them, so is this any different to other families? Would you see your son's children as much as you see your daughter's children? I know the partner's mother loves babies and looks after her grandchild while her other daughter works. So does that mean that I'm cut out of [a relationship with] the partner's child more because it's not my daughter's child but my daughter's partner's child? Or will the partner's mother take over my daughter's baby? The possibility is there but I don't think it will happen because the other grandmother and my daughter don't hit it off so well. I think that there is potential for jealousy. I think that if I look after the partner's baby more than her mum does, her mum would be jealous.

As can be seen in this interview, there are many unknowns in the situation. Some, regarding the partner's mother, are not exclusive to lesbian relationships. However, there are many pluses in Linda's situation as she already has a positive and accepting relationship with her daughter and her daughter's partner, and this is the best starting point for the grandparent relationship which, as indicated in Chapter 1, is not simply a relationship between the grandparents and grandchildren but is imbedded within a broader system of family relationships. With this strong foundation most of Linda's immediate concerns should work their way through after the birth of the first baby, and when and if the partner becomes pregnant.

Other parents and grandparents may have concerns similar to Linda's, or they may have concerns that are specific to the particular relationship of their daughter or son. Where the relationship with their own child is already difficult, including issues with their partner, grandparents are more likely to have some difficulties which may affect their relationship with their grandchild. Such difficulties also occur in conventional heterosexual family relationships. However, in the relationships between lesbian and gay parents the grandparent generation may focus on the same-sex relationship rather than other problems in the family relationships. If this is the case the grandparents will have to work through their own prejudices if they want a good relationship with their grandchild.

Grandparents may also be worried about the lack of a male parent in lesbian families, genetic heritage of their grandchild or potential grandchild, and perhaps be curious about the way in which lesbian women become pregnant. Linda's daughter used IVF because of fertility problems, but there are a number of options open to lesbians who want a child. They can use donor sperm from either a known donor who is a friend or acquaintance, or an unknown donor. They may either self-inseminate with donor sperm or in some states visit a clinic after referral by a GP. If donor sperm does not result in pregnancy the woman can be referred to a fertility specialist; if found to be medically infertile she can be referred to an IVF program. Grandparents who want to know more about the pros and cons of these choices may find the information that is prepared for potential lesbian mothers is a good source of information for them. One such resource for prospective lesbian parents is the Royal Women's Hospital (Melbourne) resource book *Pride and Joy*, and there are likely to be similar sources of information in other states.

Natalie

Natalie, a lesbian mother, made quite a different choice in her approach to motherhood from that of Linda's daughter who had fertility problems. She and her partner had decided to have a known donor so that the child could have an ongoing relationship with her father. The donor (father) regularly sees his child, a girl, and intends to continue his relationship with her. According to both the mother and the father, both sets of grandparents— parents of both partners—are very happy about the situation and all have regular contact with the toddler. The donor father's mother, who is quite elderly and who had never expected to have grandchildren because her son is gay, also has occasional contact and is reported to be very happy about her grandchild.

It is worth remembering that grandchildren with lesbian and gay parents benefit just as much as other grandchildren if they have good relationships with loving grandparents. As discussed in Chapter 1, grandparents expand their grandchildren's understanding of and exposure to many aspects of life; they are usually loving, accepting and indulgent; they teach the children different ways of looking at the world and they enrich the grand-children's knowledge of the family. Grandchildren who have a good relationship with their grandparents benefit no matter what their family situation. Grandparents, but particularly grandmothers, with a good, close relationship with their grandchildren often become alternative attachment figures for grandchildren. All grandparents who have a good relationship with their grandchildren provide a positive emotional dimension within the web of family relationships.

While the grandparents in both the above lesbian family situations are accepting of the situation, this is not the case with all grandparents, or not initially. The National Lesbian Family Study in the United States indicates that some grandparents are not understanding during the pregnancy but usually accept the baby after it is born. Only about three per cent of grandparents did not adjust in the end. By the time the children in this study were five years old, 63 per cent of the grandparents were open about their grandchild's family, while the others did not disclose to their friends that their grandchild lived in a lesbian family. This of course is an individual decision that grandparents make, but the lack of openness may hurt the feelings of their own child and her partner, and the grandchildren are less likely to benefit from the relationship with their grandparents in these circumstances especially if their grandchildren eventually become aware of the situation. On the other hand, if lesbian and gay parents themselves do not wish to disclose, grandparents should go along with this decision so that there is harmony in the family relationships.

Grandchildren in gay families are less likely to be a concern for grandparents as there are fewer gay men bringing up children. Children of gay men have usually been conceived in a heterosexual relationship with the child's mother, although there are also some gay men who have a child with a lesbian mother (as in the case discussed above); they may or may not have continuing contact with the child. A few gay men are fostering children or have had one born in a surrogacy agreement, but this is rare and there is little information available about these families.

Quite clearly grandparents who do not fully accept the family situation of grandchildren in gay and lesbian families are less likely to have close relationships with them, especially as the children grow older and become aware of and resent their lack of approval. Negative attitudes in grandparents may mean that they are not available to their grandchildren in times of crisis and that their grandchildren do not have the positive benefits that the grandchildren of more accepting grandparents receive.

Children in lesbian and gay families

Many grandparents, even though they are accepting, are likely to be concerned about the long-term wellbeing of grandchildren growing up in lesbian and gay families. More is known about the children of lesbians, whether brought up by a single lesbian mother or a couple, than about children brought up by gay men, simply because there are more of them. As indicated already, the children of gay men are more likely to be living with their mothers. This section is written specifically to allay the fears that grandparents may have about grandchildren living in same-sex families or with a single homosexual parent.

The major concern about children in lesbian families is that their psychological and social development may be negatively affected because they usually do not have the care and affection of a father. This does not of course apply to the small proportion of lesbian families where the donor father has a relationship with the child, nor does it apply to those children who were born in heterosexual relationships and continue to have a relationship with their fathers.

Other common concerns about children brought up by single lesbian women and lesbian couples are whether the children are more likely to become gay or lesbian themselves; if they will have an atypical gender identification; or if they will have low self-esteem caused by social stigma. Where the lesbian mother is single there are also fears that the children may experience social and emotional maladjustment. However, research spanning 20 years does not bear out these concerns.

Long-term studies of the children of lesbian mothers who were conceived in heterosexual relationships have revealed no significant differences between them and the children of heterosexual mothers. The children of lesbian mothers are no more likely to be gay or lesbian or to have a confused gender identity than other children. These children have self-esteem and emotional wellbeing within the usual range and their social development is also in the normal range in regard to confidence and positive peer relationships. Furthermore, they are no more likely to be teased or bullied than the children of heterosexual mothers.

There is less research on children who were conceived in lesbian relationships, but in general what little research there is confirms the above findings. The majority of studies show that children raised by lesbian and gay parents grow up as well adjusted and healthy as children raised by non-gay and lesbian parents. Nevertheless, there have been several small studies of the children of lesbian mothers that report different findings. These studies have shown that some children of lesbian mothers are willing to consider homosexuality but they do not necessarily act upon it. They are generally more affectionate and receptive and have a sense of wellbeing and contentment, but some children also fear stigma and remember being teased more. Some of these children also perceive themselves as less intelligent and physically able than children from families where there is a father present.

Grandparents should be aware that this research is not saying that fathering (and mothering in the case of gay families) is not important; rather it emphasises that what is important for positive development in children is good parenting. Much research over the years has reported that it is the quality of the relationships in the family that matter for children and the absence of ongoing conflict, no matter what the structure of the family. Parents who are nurturing, caring and loving are most important for children. Studies of lesbian mothers show that they are just as caring of their children as heterosexual mothers. Similarly, there is no reason to believe that gay men are unfit as parents.

Grandparents also need to understand that the legal issues that many lesbian (and gay) couples face affect not only the couple but also the legal status of their grandchildren, and this is of concern. These legal issues arise because the parents are unable to marry in Australia, and include the fact that the second parent is not the legal guardian of the other parent's child unless the couple take steps to overcome this situation through the Family Court or through some other legal avenue. At present there are attempts to change the law to recognise both partners as the legal parents. It is not my intention to go into all the permutations of lesbian and gay families, because the legal situations are different in the different States, and because changes to the current situation are being advocated and investigated.

Community acceptance and support for children in lesbian and gay families

Grandparents and parents can make a difference to the wellbeing not only of their gay or lesbian son or daughter but also of their grandchildren just by being accepting and supportive. It has been found in many studies that positive family and community support is linked to positive outcomes for children in all family situations. On the other hand, poor social support is linked to greater family stress and poorer outcomes for children. Gay and lesbian families are no different from other families in their need for support and acceptance both within the family network and in the wider community.

The Lesbian and Gay Families Project carried out in Victoria examined, amongst other things, the family and community supports the participants received (McNair, Dempsey, Wise & Perlesz 2002). It found that lesbian parents had quite high levels of acceptance and support from family, friendship and community networks. Children in lesbian families were also well accepted and reported few difficulties in relation to their parent's sexuality. However, although most were open with friends and work colleagues, a meaningful proportion did not disclose their situation, nor did they disclose the situation to their children's school friends or within the broader community. The greatest source of pride for participants in this study was in bringing up happy, well-adjusted children. However, their observations were that they did so despite living in a homophobic society.

Grandparents may worry about how their grandchildren in same-sex relationships experience the situation at school. An Australian study of the school experiences of the children of lesbian and gay parents found that there were age differences in children's experiences (Ray & Gregory 2001). In primary school, the younger the child, the less likely they were to keep their family circumstances to themselves. It was the older children in years 3 and

4 at primary school who more often reported keeping their family situation to themselves. By year 5 some children made up answers when asked about their family, or were reluctant to answer at all. Overall, 90 percent of the children from prep to year 6 were open about their families and their parents' sexuality. The younger children generally did not experience bullying, but just under half of the children in years 3 to 6 had experienced being bullied at some time. Sometimes taunts about gays and lesbians were used and this upset the children. This led older children to be careful about disclosure for fear of being hurt, but most of the children said that they ignored the bullies.

At secondary school over a third of the children in years 7 to 10 did not disclose the sexuality of their parents to other children, but students in years 11 and 12 were more open and 86 per cent disclosed because they considered that their peers were more mature. They tended to be selective about telling their friends and felt that questions were a positive sign. Like the children in primary school fewer than half the secondary students had experienced bullying and teasing at some time but this declined as they got older and by the time they reached years 11 and 12 only 14 per cent reported having had this negative experience.

Generally, children of all ages in this study said that there were advantages in being the children of lesbian and gay parents. Some felt that they were special and proud to be different; some were pleased to be part of the gay community; some to have two 'mums', and all felt that it was good to get together with other children in similar families. The secondary school students thought that they were more open-minded. On the other hand, although this study did not involve large numbers of children, they did report that schools did not handle the problem of homophobia in a way that made them feel safe.

Although these studies show that there are positive outcomes for children in lesbian and gay families it does not mean that grandchildren will not have some bad experiences in a community where there is still discrimination despite legal and policy changes that support acceptance. Grandparents who are not so directly involved in the situation can be a great support to their grandchildren at such times and help them talk through their difficulties and give advice, or just provide loving acceptance and support.

This, however, will depend on the quality and closeness of the relationship they have with their grandchildren.

Grandchildren with disabilities

As discussed in Chapter 1, most grandparents anticipate the birth of a grandchild with pleasure and enjoy the process of getting to know each new grandchild and watching their development. Most enjoy time with their grandchildren and find their role satisfying, and many gain a sense of personal fulfilment and family renewal. When a grandchild is born with a disability or is diagnosed later, these satisfactions may be more difficult to achieve.

There is very little written on grandparents' roles and reactions to having a grandchild with a disability, but grandparents can benefit from information about the pattern of reactions of parents so that they are more understanding of the process involved and can support them appropriately. I have had the opportunity of interviewing a number of mothers of children with disabilities, and their views of the grandparents' roles and reactions are included in this discussion of the issues.

Much is known about the reactions of parents who have a child with a disability. When a child is diagnosed with a disability, whether at birth or later, parents grieve for the loss of the healthy child they had anticipated. However, there are some differences in these reactions depending on the type and degree of disability and the extent to which it is affecting the everyday life of the child and other family members. This sorrow goes through several states of grieving, which have no time limits and may often overlap. These include loss, denial, anxiety, guilt, depression, anger, rejection, isolation, hopelessness, resentment and antagonism. As parents begin to confront the reality of the situation they also begin to accept their child's limitations. Parents may experience this grief repeatedly as other children reach specific developmental milestones such as walking, talking, starting school, reaching adolescence and so on. There is also evidence that the marriage of parents can be put under pressure and that some parents, often fathers, do not accept the disability.

Research indicates that the intensity of grief felt by parents may differ depending on the number, sex and age of siblings, the nature and visibility of the disability, the coping strategies of family members, the stability of the marriage and the amount of support they receive. One of my own grandchildren has talipes (club feet) and had an operation, plaster and splints in the first year of life and will face this procedure again next year. Nevertheless, because the prognosis for this condition is so good, this disability is accepted within the family without any great grief; rather it is regretted that this child will have to experience the pain and discomfort of another operation and plaster. During the post-operative period while the child is in plaster and splints it will be harder to ignore the disability, but we all know that this will be temporary.

Parents of children with disabilities often experience more stress in their parenting than other parents, depending on the disability. There are additional care-giving demands as more time is often needed with routine tasks such as feeding, bathing and dressing. Support by relatives, friends and the community is especially important to the families of children with disabilities and the greater the level of support received—especially informal support—the lower the level of stress. It has been found that mothers of children with disabilities spend twice as much time in caretaking as the mothers of typical children, and unfortunately fathers do not always share the care. But as I indicated earlier, it depends to a great extent on the nature of the disability.

The cultural background of the family sometimes affects the parents' acceptance of their child's disability. It may also affect their understanding of inclusion in preschool, child care and schooling. In some cultures a child with a disability may stigmatise the family and be seen as retribution for past sins and even the sins of family ancestors.

Grandparents may go through some of the same reactions as parents at diagnosis but they are also likely to be distressed because of the reactions of their own child (the child's parent) and their partner. They are also concerned about the effects, both immediate and in the longer term, on any siblings; they can provide important support to these grandchildren who may need extra attention.

I discussed the role of grandparents with a focus group of mothers of preschool children with disabilities who attended an early intervention centre. They barely mentioned grandfathers; they focused on the roles of grandmothers. Their experiences of the support provided were mixed, both good and bad. Some found that grandmothers were a great help; others said that they did not support them much at all; and others did not have contact because they lived too far away or had died. The following is a list of the varied reactions of grandmothers as reported by mothers:

- She [my mother; the grandmother] backed right away because she was too scared to deal with the grandchild's disabilities and such things as giving medication. She also has eight very healthy grandchildren who take up her time.

- She gets depressed about it but doesn't live close so she can't really help.

- She thought an 'operation would fix it'. [The child's disabilities were severe and multiple.]

- One mother said that her mother [the grandmother] didn't want to be seen as 'bossy' by telling her daughter what to do. She was only 'kind of supportive' but mostly it was just the mother herself who found the supports, both information and services, by driving around and knocking on doors.

- One mother, who had a child with a feeding tube and multiple disabilities, had a wonderful mother-in-law who, although she did not live close by, stayed with her for four months when her son was born prematurely and very ill. She said, 'She was my "rock" and my only support. She cleaned and looked after everybody when our child was born and looked after my older daughter who was very distressed.'

- Sometimes grandparents and other family members believed that autistic children were just badly behaved and that it was due to bad parenting.

Constance, a grandmother who has a grandson now aged 16 with Down syndrome, has been through some of the reactions to her grandson's disability that are discussed above in regards to parents. Here are her comments about his birth:

Constance

> I felt devastated because I had spoken to the parents about having the test for Down syndrome. However, they [the parents] did not have it done because their first child was very premature and this test can cause babies to be born prematurely. So when he was born it was all unexpected. I was grieving for both my son and the child. At first it was grief and then I was very angry. I didn't know (at first) why they didn't have this test, which is why it was such a shock. However, the parents were really very good about it. So then we settled down and became interested and thought, perhaps it's not so bad. When he was a few months old his eyes started to roll around in his head but as time went on the eldest child was very thrilled with him and he just settled down into the family.

Constance could not care for the boy much when he was a baby because he was breast-fed, but when he was a little older she cared for him when she could, and continues to do so now that he is a teenager. He now goes to a special school and she picks him up after school and takes him to her home. He is quite happy there and his mother picks him up later. Constance explained: 'We were really relieved when Noah's Ark [an Early Intervention Service] was able to help his mother with feeding and so on.' She said that she did not seem to revisit the grief as he grew older; she just accepted him the way he was. 'His mother was very brave and had another baby, and that helped to settle things down. I have had him and his siblings down at our little shack at the beach on their own. It has settled over time.' However, Constance, like many grandparents and parents, worries about the future for the child now that he is in his teens.

Constance got over her first negative reactions to her grandson and has been a great support to the family. She has a good, loving relationship with her grandson and is also a support to his siblings. However, these positive relationships exist on the foundation of a good relationship with both her son and daughter-in-law and this is the key fact.

Another mother who has a severely disabled baby is in a rather different situation; she explained that her father—the grandfather of the child and with whom she has a very close relationship—had reacted very negatively when her son was born with multiple disabilities. The grandfather had hoped that the child would not live, and was totally negative about him because he did not want to see his daughter weighed down by the needs of such a disabled baby. However, he has changed his attitude and is now his daughter's greatest support as she struggles to get the services and supports she needs to care for her son.

It is not the end of the world if grandparents initially have negative reactions to grandchildren with disabilities. They are concerned about the effect that it will have on their own child's life and family as well as the effects on the grandchild. Time helps acceptance with them as it does with the parents. Where grandparents have a good relationship with the parents they can assist in the process of acceptance through the provision of appropriate support. Nevertheless, according to mothers of young children with disabilities, there is a need for more education about disabilities, not only for grandparents but also for the broader community.

Death of a grandchild

I had not originally intended to write about death in this book as the focus is on the grandparent's relationships with the younger generations and the issues involved. However death is part of the life cycle and can occur at any age, so should not be omitted from our discussion. What brought the issue to my attention was finding articles on the Internet which described the personal experiences of grandparents who had lost a much-loved grandchild through death. Reading their expressions of grief and loss moved me deeply, and also made me realise how fragile life is, even for the young. When a loved grandchild dies the parents are devastated by grief, but the situation for grandparents is not any less painful and is less straightforward.

The grief of grandparents is not always considered when a grandchild dies. There is often an assumption that grandparents are not as affected by the death as are the parents, because they are a generation removed. However, this is not true if the grandparents have had a close and loving relationship with the grandchild. It is also sometimes thought that because grandparents are from an older generation that they are more experienced with death, dying and grief, and therefore do not need support and understanding in the way that parents do.

In these days of modern medicine and increased longevity, neither grandparents nor parents expect their children or grandchildren to die before them. The death of a grandchild affects not only the parents and grandparents but the whole of the extended family, including siblings of the child and siblings of the parents. Because of the magnitude of the parents' loss there is immediate sympathy and support; much is written on the grief of parents, but this is not so for grandparents. Yet the grandparents are suffering in a way that is doubled, because they grieve not only for their lost grandchild but also for their son or daughter's loss and suffering. Grandparents cannot fix things for their own child as they did when they were young; they cannot kiss them better and they cannot buy them a new toy to replace the broken one; a child is not replaceable.

The following excerpt from a much longer poem, 'For bereaved grandparents' by Margaret H. Gerber, expresses some of the feelings of a grandmother for her own daughter after the death of her grand-daughter Emily, aged three.

> I am powerlessness. I am helplessness. I am frustration.
> I sit with her and I cry with her.
> She cries for her daughter and I cry for mine.
> I can't help her.
> I can't reach inside her and take her broken heart.
> I must watch her suffer day after day.
> (Reproduced with permission from Margaret H Gerber from her book, *For Bereaved Grandparents*, 1990, Centering Corporation, Omaha, Nebraska.)

Grandparents may also struggle with the notion that the death is contrary to the natural order, and some may have to cope with survival guilt because they are old and the child young. The death of a grandchild brings to a halt the hopes and expectations that grandparents may have had for the future in relation to this child and the next generation of their family.

Most of the information about the effects of the death of a grandchild comes from practical counselling sources and personal experience. The exception to this is a small qualitative study in the United States of nine grandmothers who were aged from 40 to 83 years of age (Galinsky 2003). The grandchildren were aged from 28 weeks in utero to 18 years; the time since the deaths ranged from two months to 17 years, and the causes of death were varied. It was found that both the actual funeral and the arrangements for the funeral set the tone for relationships and communication between the generations after the funeral. The families that coped best had planned the funeral together. Most of the grandparents did not talk to their families about their grief, but most of the married grandmothers received support from their husbands. The grandmothers who did not receive this support were more distressed. Most grandmothers did not seek counselling and the reason given by the two who did so was that they needed to validate their responses to the experience. One grandparent attended a bereavement support group but was uncomfortable at being the only grandparent attending. She thought that separate groups for grandparents would have been more useful. The grandmothers also complained that there was little to read about grandparents' reactions to the death of a grandchild and few places where they could talk about their reactions and grief.

Grandparents usually try to provide support for the parents of the child, especially to their own child, while trying to keep their own grief under wraps. They want to protect their own child as much as possible and some grandparents may step in and take control when they see their child collapsing with the weight of grief. Other grandparents may try not to interfere. A funeral director writing in the journal *Forum*, which is produced by the Association for Death Education and Counselling, points out that grandparents have a great need to remain strong for their child, but he has seen some grandparents take this need too far. He has also seen cases where the grandparents take over from the parents, and on some occasions he has seen the two sets of grandparents from different sides of the family compete to 'rescue' the parents and in doing so add to the stress. Often there is no place where grandparents can talk about their own grieving without upsetting other members of the family. Grieving has no set time period and may continue for years. Finding peers or others who are accepting of their distress is important not only for parents but also for grandparents.

Grandparents who understand the situation of other grandparents are likely to be the best supports for grandparents who are grieving for their grandchild and their own child.

Conclusions

The three different family circumstances described in this chapter all involve a process of loss and a challenge to expectations. Change and difference are always stressful until the situation is accepted. With the diagnosis of a grandchild's disability, grandparents and parents may experience grief and distress before they accept a situation that cannot be changed, although they may still continue to worry about the future of the child. Acceptance of children and parents in lesbian or gay families is necessary for all concerned in order to have positive relationships with grandchildren in these families, and for the grandchildren to experience the positive benefits of their relationship with their grandparents. The grandparents' role in both these circumstances remains important to both the grandchildren and the parents.

The death of a grandchild, on the other hand, is something that all grandparents hope will not happen and the loss is great. What is clear in each of these family situations is that support and understanding, both within the family network as well as within the wider community, is important for the wellbeing of all concerned.

References

Centre for Community Child Health 2002a, *A framework to develop the social dimensions of disability: a report prepared for Noah's Ark*, Melbourne.

Centre for Community Child Health 2002b, *New frontiers in early childhood inclusion: a report prepared for Noah's Ark*, Melbourne.

Easthope, T 2003, 'Grandparent grief: "nipped in the bud"', *The Forum*, Association for Death Education and Counselling, West Hartford.

Fitzgerald, H 2004, *The grief of grandparents*, American Hospice Foundation, Washington.

Galinsky, N 2003, 'The death of a grandchild: a complex grief', *The Forum*, Association for Death Education and Counselling, West Hartford.

Gartrell, N, Banks, A, Hamilton, J, Reed, N, Bishop, H & Rodas, C 1999, 'The national lesbian family study: 2: interviews with mothers of toddlers', *American Journal of Orthopsychiatry*, vol. 69, no. 3, pp. 362–9.

Gartrell, N, Banks, A, Reed, N, Hamilton, J, Rodas, C & Deck, A 2000, 'The national lesbian family study: 2: interviews with mothers of five-year-olds', *American Journal of Orthopsychiatry*, vol. 70, no. 4, pp. 542–8.

Gerber, MH 1990, *For bereaved grandparents*, Centering Corporation, Omaha, Nebraska.

Hamner, T & Turner, P 1996, *Parenting in contemporary society*, 3rd edn, Allyn & Bacon, Boston.

McNair, R, Dempsey, D, Wise, S & Perlesz, A 2002, 'Lesbian parenting: issues, strengths and challenges', *Family Matters*, no. 63, pp. 40–9.

Patterson, C 1995, *Lesbian and gay parenting*, American Psychological Association ONLINE, viewed 9 March 2006, (http://www.apa.org/pi/parent.html).

Ray, V & Gregory, R 2001, 'School experiences of the children of lesbian and gay parents', *Family Matters*, Australian Institute of Family Studies, Melbourne.

Reed, ML 2003, 'Grandparents' grief—who is listening?', *The Forum*, Association for Death Education and Counselling, West Hartford.

Rickard, M 2002, *Children of lesbian and single women parents*, Research Note 41, Department of the Parliamentary Library, Canberra.

Robertson, P 2003, 'Report on Lesbian Health Research Centre salon on grandparenting', Lesbian Health Research Centre, University of California, San Francisco.

Chapter 6

Child development and parenting

Grandparents are often concerned about the way in which their grandchildren are being parented and find that many things that they did when bringing up their own children are now frowned upon. I have found that although I have professional knowledge about parenting and child development issues I can still make mistakes in the eyes of my children. Many changes have occurred in parenting and many grandparents feel confused, so this chapter provides information to make it easier for them to understand some of the current issues and attitudes.

One of the things that concern some grandparents is the behaviour of grandchildren and what many people call 'discipline'. Disagreement over the way that children are being parented can cause conflict between the parent and grandparent generations if grandparents try to interfere or give too much 'advice'. But the reverse is sometimes true; parents can be displeased with the way that the grandparents manage their grandchildren's behaviour, especially when they are caring for grandchildren on a regular basis and sometimes they can be quite critical. Some parents believe that the grandparents are too indulgent and allow the grandchildren to do what they like or, on the other hand, that the grandparents are too strict.

A grandfather who was interviewed for an earlier chapter in this book, and who has professional expertise in child development, told me how, when he was a parent, he had been annoyed with his own parents over the way they had indulged his children.

Robert

> When my kids were younger I used to get into terrible fights with my parents. I'd say, 'That's wrong; that's not the way; you're undermining me, etc.' I went on and on. I realise now how stupid that was. If I had my time all over again I would realise that's exactly what grandparents are there for, to spoil them. No harm is going to come out of it for the great majority of kids. Kids are also better behaved for grandparents than they are for parents.

This grandfather indulges his grandchildren, just as his parents did, and gains great pleasure from their company and in seeing them grow and learn.

On the other hand, a mother who was interviewed for another project had the opposite experience. Her mother came to stay to help out after the birth of her second child but was so strict with the older grandchild that he was very unhappy. Eventually the grandmother was encouraged to go home; it was a very unpleasant experience for everyone. However, the evidence suggests that grandparents are more likely to be indulgent with grandchildren than overly severe.

Parents may be bringing up their children quite differently from the way they were brought up themselves, and this may be confusing, and even hurtful, to some grandparents. The difference may be because they did not like the way their parents raised them, but it is more likely to be because they realise that their children are growing up in a very changed world and that their needs are different, and that ideas about bringing up children have changed.

Migrant parents and grandparents often have a dilemma as they try to balance their own traditions and customs with Australian ways. They want their children and grandchildren to take advantage of the opportunities available in Australia but also to maintain the traditions of their own culture. But children have minds of their own and are influenced by the families that they mix with in the community and by their experiences at school, and so they may reject some aspects of the old country and its culture despite the efforts of the older generations.

One of the major changes is that much more is known about children's development, and in particular brain development, in the early years of life.

Research on the brains of babies and young children has led to greater and more serious concern with setting good foundations in the early years of life. Parents and grandparents may come across information about this research in the media and may worry whether they are doing the right thing. Anxiety about 'doing the right thing' is ever present and is perhaps exacerbated because families are smaller, with usually only one or two children, and because the parents are often older when they finally have children.

Parents increasingly seek help with their parenting through books and magazines, through listening to 'experts' on the radio and television and/or attending parenting classes. Many of them are anxious about their parenting and this may seem strange to some grandparents who 'just did it', as one of the grandmothers I interviewed told me. All States in Australia provide various kinds of support for parents, including universally available advice for new mothers and babies, parenting classes, tip sheets on various aspects of parenting, support groups for new mothers, and playgroups for children where parents learn informally how to manage their children's behaviour and a little about child development. The consequence of all this seeking of information about parenting is that grandparents also want to know more so that there is consistency and harmony in the family, and also to see if any of their reservations about the way their grandchildren are being brought up have any validity.

While there are many sources of information for parents, there are few that directly address the concerns of grandparents. Various organisations are attempting to fill this gap by running grandparent support groups and providing advice to grandparents who are having difficulties with some of the issues which have been discussed in this book. Where grandparents join parenting groups that are designed for parents, it often does not work out well, as the needs and interests of the parents and those of the grandparents are different, and the grandparents may appear critical of the parents. The few groups which are available specifically for grandparents reach only a minority and, in any case, not all grandparents want to join a group. However, there is an increasing amount of advice for grandparents available on the Internet, for those who have access to computers and the skill to use them.

To help grandparents understand why changes in parenting and child rearing have occurred, the next section deals with positive approaches to the management of children's behaviour, rather than physical punishment such as smacking. Following that is some information about recent research on child development and the implications of research on the brain. Finally, there is a discussion about parenting education, and a listing and discussion of the major transitions in childhood which are often the focus for providing information for parents. The implications of this information for grandparents is discussed.

Behaviour management

One of the continuing issues in child rearing and the education of children is corporal punishment. When I was a child and later when I was a young primary teacher, corporal punishment was commonplace in schools and in many homes. The severity of the punishment varied from a slap on the leg or the bottom, to the strap or cane at school, or sometimes a 'good thrashing' at home. These days corporal punishment is generally banned in schools and used much less by parents. However it is still a bone of contention and the issues are often misunderstood.

It is difficult not only for parents but also for some grandparents to understand that there are ways to manage inappropriate behaviour in children other than punishment, and especially corporal punishment. Grandparents may not want to be harsh with their grandchildren themselves but still may think that the parents should 'discipline' them more.

Although the norms of our society are now against extreme forms of physical punishment there is still widespread acceptance of moderate and reasonable use of physical force. Many parents continue to smack their children and do not see anything wrong with a slap or smack when children are being difficult. Some parents feel strongly that it is their right to smack their children, while others feel just as strongly that smacking or any form of physical punishment of children is wrong. Grandparents are also likely to have views about smacking that are just as mixed as those of the parents, but even when they do not think that smacking is wrong, they are much less likely to actually smack or physically punish their grandchildren simply because their relationship with their grandchildren is usually much more indulgent and accepting.

There are many arguments against the physical punishment of children:

- that it contravenes the rights of children
- that it is an assault on children in the name of punishment
- that it is an insult to the dignity of the child
- that it is ineffective in changing children's behaviour
- that it is associated with child abuse if parents go too far, especially with children under the age of two.

On the other hand, the reasons for continuing to allow physical punishment include biblical injunctions and beliefs, and beliefs that such punishment is necessary where dangerous or anti-social behaviour is involved. Some parents also believe that physical punishment had been good for them as children, and so continue to use it with their own children.

The best review of the issues involved is Penelope Leach's article 'Spanking: a short cut to nowhere', which puts the arguments against smacking in the context not only of children's development, but also of children's own feelings when they are smacked. Leach is a well-known British expert on child development and the author of a number of excellent books on child development (see the reference section of this chapter). She argues that the major argument against physical punishment is that it is ineffective and does not achieve the outcomes that parents want, which is to stop the unwanted bad or annoying behaviour of their child. Leach is an advocate for the wellbeing of babies and children, and what makes her arguments unique and effective is that they are told from the perspective of the child.

Leach argues that parents spank because they think it will teach children not to do things that are naughty, or it will stop them when they are being a nuisance and grizzly. Most parents realise that children have to learn to behave well so that they get on with other family members and also with other children and adults outside the home at preschool, school, and elsewhere. Good parents know that it is in the child's own interests to get on with other children and to be welcome in settings other than their own home. Many parents think spanking will encourage children to behave better not only at home but in other settings, but the evidence does not bear this out.

Leach cites research evidence that many parents start smacking children before they are one year old, and many more do so before the children are four years old, but research has shown that it does not make for better behaved preschool children in the long run. Research on older children indicates that those who were physically punished at school did not improve their behaviour and that they continued to receive repeated physical punishments for similar bad behaviour.

Many people feel that violence against children is far removed from what goes on in their family when children receive a smack or a slap which they believe teaches them not to misbehave. But smacks and slaps, which are often only given to relieve the parent's feelings of frustration, are ineffective, as the child usually responds by crying and continuing to be exasperating. There is always the danger that although the original slap is considered 'reasonable punishment', some parents may go one step further in their frustration with a child. Using physical punishment can arouse aggressive feelings in the person administering it, and most parents who are prosecuted for abusing their children have wanted to be good parents but after using force, when it failed to have the desired results, followed by more force and eventually 'went too far'.

Leach has found that young children usually have no idea why they were smacked other than that their parent was cross or that they were bad, but in comparison they remember the actual punishment clearly. The parent may have told them exactly why they were smacked, but the reasons get lost in the feelings invoked. These feelings differ depending on the age of the children involved. For example, a baby or toddler is horrified that the person that they love best has hurt them, and often turn to them for comfort; they do not have the capacity to understand. The preschool child is usually overwhelmed with anger and will try to take it out on someone else; older children are angry but also humiliated. The self-esteem of older children suffers more than their body. These young children do not focus on what they have done to cause the punishment; they are caught up in their own reactions to it, and the tiny ones do not understand at all because they have not reached the stage of development that will allow them to understand. One of the worst aspects of physical punishment for children who are modelling themselves on adult behaviour is that it teaches them that aggression can be used to solve problems, and this can lead to aggressive behaviour.

Some knowledge of how children learn to behave may help grandparents to understand what to do when young children are difficult. Leach argues that this is the best way to learn how to manage children's behaviour and to use alternatives to smacking.

Learning to behave

Children are not born knowing how to behave; they learn it from their parents and those around them, including grandparents and other family members, and they have an inbuilt desire to learn. Babies love their parents and want to please them, but they can only learn at their own developmental pace physically, intellectually and emotionally, so adults must always take this into account. Expecting too much of a baby, toddler or young child will make him or her unhappy, and ultimately uncooperative, especially if they fear the loss of love.

The following is a summary of the points that Leach makes about how children learn to behave at different ages from infancy to the early years of primary school. The foundations for children's behaviour as adolescents and young adults are laid in these early years, so these are important times for all children. This section is followed by some suggestions for positive discipline without resort to smacking or other physical punishments.

- *Babies*: Babies do not have the capacity to understand the feelings of others, no matter what they are doing, whether crying or waking in the middle of the night. They are not trying to upset their parents or any other care giver; it is just the way they feel at the time.

- *Toddlers*: Toddlers are driven by their curiosity to explore the world around them. It is integral to their development but sometimes difficult for those around them that they do not learn what is unacceptable only by being told once or twice. It will take time—probably months—but they will eventually learn what is acceptable and what is not. Two-year-olds are not 'good' or 'naughty' on purpose; they do not know what the difference is. They want to do things for themselves but also want the comfort of cuddles when their own demands and temper make the world seem scary. It is easier to make a game of what you want them to do than to make demands about what they should be doing. Adults can arrange for toddlers to be 'good' by the way they approach them; for example, making a game out of having them pick up their toys. A little imagination on the part of parents, grandparents and other adults goes a long way in managing the behaviour of toddlers.

- *Preschool children*: Unlike toddlers, three- and four-year-olds understand that adults have feelings too and will also remember, at least to some degree, your instructions. They will also be able to see the results of many of their actions. At this stage children can choose whether to be good or naughty and the choice largely depends on how they feel about their parents (and other care-givers). When they have a loving and approving relationship with their parents or substitute care-giver they want to please them and therefore want to behave although, of course, there will be times when they lapse. Where children feel that they can never please their parents or care-givers they cease to try.

- *Schoolchildren*: By five, six, or seven years of age children know how to behave but they do not always do so, sometimes because, like all people, they are in an 'off' mood, and sometimes because they make mistakes as they still have a lot to learn. Children in this age group can vary in behaviour from being sweet and caring to being difficult, insolent and using bad language. They need explanations about what is acceptable behaviour but they also need reassurance that, while certain behaviours are unacceptable, they are still loved and wanted.

Positive discipline for managing children's behaviour

Children learn better through cooperative approaches and rewards than through punishment and force. Rewards do not have to be objects such as toys or lollies; children mainly want the attention of their parents or any other person that they care about, including grandparents. This is the main reward for young children. Some parents fear giving too much attention to their children for fear of spoiling them, and often inadvertently give naughty children more attention than cooperative children who are less demanding. The ones who are spoilt are the children who blackmail their parents into giving them things to stop their bad behaviour. Children who are given attention and treats because they are cooperative and enjoyable to be with are not spoilt children.

Parents are the most important people in children's lives. Children model themselves on their parents and will copy their parents and take more notice of what parents *do* rather than what they *say*. Children watch their parents' behaviour in relation to other people, and will notice cooperation, politeness and honesty. Penelope Leach suggests that parents should be honest with their children when they are angry or tired, and should explain their reasons for certain behaviour or actions so that children can learn from experience and observation. She also points out that *do* works better than *don't* in managing behaviour. Leach makes the following suggestions to parents, which apply equally to grandparents, in order to avoid conflict when caring for young children at different ages:

- *Babies*: Baby-proof and make safe living areas to reduce conflict over dangerous items. Put breakables out of reach. Grab children's hands away from danger rather than slapping. If parents or grandparents feel their temper is getting out of control they should put the baby in a safe place such as a cot or playpen and leave the room, even if the child cries. It's safer to leave for a brief time so that you can cool down, than to stay and risk hitting out.

- *Toddlers*: Avoid direct clashes by finding distractions and diversions. Carry the child or pick them up when they are heading for something dangerous. Try not to join in with tantrums. Parents can sing, turn their backs, or if in public, remove the child to the nearest private place when they start to tantrum. Recognise that toddlers cannot play safely by themselves. They need some fun with parents or other care-givers and need a sharp watch kept on all their activities.

- *Older children*: Much of what applies to toddlers also applies in avoiding confrontations with older children. However, when things are getting out of control, get down to the level of children who are behaving in silly or provoking ways, hold their arms firmly, and talk to them directly face-to-face so that they cannot avoid hearing what is said. Parents (or grandparents) can also remove themselves from sources of tension for five minutes of cooling off. If the child needs punishment it should be appropriately related to the 'crime' and happen at the time the event occurs.

As children get older and reach an age of understanding, allowing the logical consequences of inappropriate behaviour to occur is a much better approach than punishment unless the child is doing something dangerous. Praise and rewards, on the other hand, promote a positive self concept in children and motivate children to learn.

In taking a positive approach to discipline there is very little mention of punishment. It is regrettable that these days 'discipline' and 'punishment' are often used synonymously. When talking about discipline, many people actually mean punishment, however, the word 'discipline' derives from 'disciple'—someone who is led, a follower—and 'discipline' means leading or guiding others. Used correctly, the word 'discipline' means a positive system of guidance for children, with methods of punishment as only a small part of the scheme. Grandparents, especially those with a close bond to grandchildren, have many opportunities to provide guidance for their grandchildren and in many different ways. Discipline, especially with young children, is more appropriately thought of as behaviour management.

Current thinking about children's development

The major change which has affected the way in which children are brought up is a greater understanding of children's development from birth and even before. We know a lot more about babies now, and we recognise that they are not the totally helpless little beings that was once thought. Babies can hear before birth, and are aware of the rhythms of their mother's life. We know that babies are social beings from birth and will react to their parents' voices and faces. Babies are also attracted to other people and although they prefer people they know, over the first few weeks babies gradually become more actively friendly and enjoy 'chats' with people who engage with them in face-to-face communication. Grandparents who realise this and have the opportunity to 'chat' with their new grandchild are well on the way to developing a positive relationship which will benefit both grandparents and grandchild.

Realising that not only do babies communicate from birth but that they have a range of other abilities makes it much easier for grandparents to establish a bond with a new grandchild, providing they have regular contact. Babies come into the world wanting to find out how things work. They want to make things happen and master their environment as much as they can. They can turn their heads away from or towards a stimulus such as a bright light or sound; they can follow a slowly moving object with head and eye movements; from a very young age, if well supported, they will reach out for an object in front of them and although they will not be able to grasp it for some months, they can position their hands appropriately. Babies will also let you know what they don't like in their physical world, not only by crying but by swiping and grabbing.

As children grow they are developing in several interrelated domains: the physical, intellectual, social and emotional, and each of these domains is complex in itself. Children do not develop in each developmental domain at the same rate, and while development is to some extent age-related, there are no set time periods for reaching particular developmental stages. Parents and grandparents often worry unnecessarily if they think that their children or grandchildren have not reached a particular developmental stage that some other baby or child of the same age has reached. Children's development is individual. One of my grandchildren did not crawl until quite a bit later than other babies the same age; he just could not get his bottom off the ground at the same time as the front of his body, but it has not made any difference in the long term; he is now as agile and physically well coordinated as his peers.

We know from research that one of the key elements to positive development is the sensitivity of the relationship between parents and other care-givers and the child. Relationships are the building blocks of healthy development. Grandparents who develop close, caring and accepting relationships with grandchildren are adding positively to their development and this can start at birth. Grandparents who are not as close to their grandchildren—or to some of their grandchildren—can still play a role as a part of the system of family relationships which make the grandchildren feel that they belong to something larger than a nuclear family.

There has been a long argument about 'nature' versus 'nurture' in regards to children's developmental outcomes and abilities. For a long time some people thought that the child was shaped by the environment. A major influence on the importance of the environment was the nineteenth-century British philosopher John Locke, who believed that children were born *tabula rasa*, which meant that their minds were a 'blank slate'—that they were shaped entirely by experience (Ochiltree & Edgar 1981). He emphasised the importance of *nurture* and that children should be free to explore the world.

In the 1920s the American psychologists JB Skinner and BF Watson developed a theory of conditioned behaviour usually known as behaviourism. By this they meant that desired behaviour in children should be reinforced, and that parents and others must train children in suitable behaviour. They did not believe in heredity and put the full responsibility for how children turned out on the environment and the way mothers trained their children; the emphasis was on *nurture*. The influence of behaviourism was particularly strong in the United States but also spread to other countries. The implications of behaviourism at the time were that discipline should be strict and that parents should not spoil their children. Early training in sleeping, feeding and toileting was seen as important for the development of character.

The opposing argument was that the child was determined by biology; this theory emphasised the biological importance of inheritance and nature. This perspective was promoted by science and particularly influenced thinking concerning the intelligence and talent of children; it denied the influence of nurture and the environment. These days science, and especially brain science (discussed below), has confirmed the importance of both nature and nurture in children's development; they are no longer seen as mutually exclusive but as interactive.

Recent research into the growth and development of the brains of infants and young children provides the strongest evidence that the interaction of biology and environment—that is, both nature and nurture—affects children's development (Plomin & Loehlin 1985; Shonkoff & Phillips 2000).

The early years of life have long been seen as an important stage in child development, but recent research on the brain, which is 'hard' science rather than simply theory or psychology, has meant that more significant attention is being paid to the early childhood years. Neuro-science has demonstrated that children's brains are not fully developed at birth in either size or activity. Brain growth and the development of neural pathways is not simply genetically determined but occurs as a result of interaction with the family environment. It is related to children's opportunities for exploration and trying things out, and to positive relationships with parents and other caring adults.

The National Scientific Council on the Development of the Child (in the United States) systematically analysed and synthesised the most recent research on young children's development, including brain research. Their series of working papers on this research point out how important relationships are to children's development. The initial relationship with mother, the responsiveness and warmth, the give and take of smiles and vocalisation, cuddles and play—these are all central to learning as well as to emotional wellbeing. Young children also benefit from secure nurturing relationships with other trusted adults, including grandparents, but their relationships with their parents remain the primary and central attachment. Relationships are the main feature of the children's environment, and are the foundations of their development.

Developmental psychobiology shows that children respond to the environment in ways which depend partly on their hereditary pre-dispositions. In other words, brain growth occurs in interaction between the child's genetic inheritance and their particular environment. Throughout life new experiences trigger brain growth, the development of new pathways, and the 'rewiring' of existing pathways. Excessive stress experienced by severely abused and/or neglected children may adversely affect the growth and development of the brain. However, grandparents should take heart that most of the early experiences on which brain development depends are common to most families.

Although brain development and learning continue throughout life there are 'prime times' which are important for children's development and it is important that any sensory impairment is diagnosed and treated as early as possible. Heredity contributes to individual differences in the development of children even when they live in the same family; they respond to the environment in their own individual ways. Studies of twins and adopted children have shown that environmental influences, including parenting, can moderate the inherited tendencies of children (Shonkoff & Phillips 2000). Heredity is not destiny, and the family environment and other people who have close contact with a child have a strong influence on that child's development.

Neuro-scientists and researchers in related fields of science are continuing their research on brain development (Newby & Andrew 2005). The latest research indicates that from early adolescence the brain is pruning unused neural pathways that have not been reinforced. It has also been found that this age group has difficulties in impulse control; this can be observed in scans of the brain in operation during experiments when young people have quick decisions to make. This is perhaps not surprising to those of you in close contact with adolescents and youth, who have seen examples of their impulsiveness and lack of control.

Risk and protective factors in development

Grandparents who know that one or more of their grandchildren is living in difficult family circumstances may be very worried about their wellbeing and development. Where grandchildren are living with parents who are drug addicted or alcoholic, who have a mental illness, or where there are some other circumstances that make their family environment far from ideal, grandparents may be depressed after reading about the importance of the environment and relationships. However, learning something about the development of resilience and the role that they can play in this may provide some comfort.

Grandparents will be interested and reassured to hear about the protective factors that research has found which are associated with the development of resilience in children. Resilience is the capacity to withstand stressors, to overcome adversity, to achieve positive self-esteem and appropriate levels of self-control. Resilient children deal with life transitions more smoothly, and recover from stressful events in more appropriate ways than less resilient children. Research on resilience indicates that despite the presence of risk factors, the major protective factors are:

- an easy temperament in the child
- an affectionate relationship with the main care-giver in the first year of life
- the presence of a caring adult, for example, a grandparent
- external sources of support, including grandparents, a supportive teacher, a supportive school environment, etc., which encourage and reinforce coping
- the child's ability to emotionally distance himself or herself from a bad situation which cannot be changed (such as family difficulties)
- encouragement of participation and connection with others in the community, and
- the absence of any major disability or illness in the child.

Some of these protective factors such as an easy temperament and the absence of any illness or disability in the child cannot be controlled externally as they are given factors. This means that some children are more at risk than others in a bad family environment and may need more support than others. Other protective factors, which are environmental, can be controlled to some extent within the family setting. It is also worth remembering that even addicted mothers (or parents) may be loving and warm in the first year of life and that this is a good start for their children even though a stable family environment and secure relationships are not sustained.

Grandparents, just by being there as caring adults in children's lives, can support the development of resilience in their grandchildren. They can also support their grandchildren by encouraging their participation in community organisations and events, and by helping them to weather difficult times and supporting them through transitions in their lives. They can also encourage them and advise them in the things that they are interested in, and focus on their personal strengths. Patricia in Chapter 2 is one such grandmother who is trying to support her two-year-old grand-daughter. Both the girl's parents have psychiatric illnesses and the family environment is far from stable, but the child has several protective factors including an easy temperament and the support of her grandmother.

Parent education and key transition points in the lives of children and families

Some grandparents may wonder what parent education is all about, although they know that there are changes in understanding of child development. At the time when many current grandparents had young children, parent education was not usually available in the form of parenting groups, and they just did the best they could. I know I used my copy of Doctor Spock's *Baby and Child Care* as my main source of information and education as I am sure other grandparents did.

The concept of parent education which developed in the twentieth century has become more popular in the last two or three decades. The general objective is to make parents more self-aware and confident as parents, and to improve their capacity to nurture and support their children. Over time, with more information available about children's development, the focus of 'good' parenting has changed from a more rigid approach focussed on training to a more child-centred and developmentally appropriate responsive approach to parent–child relationships. Although there was no formal parent education available in earlier times, there was still plenty of advice for parents, usually mothers, as far back as the time of Plato, however until recently this advice was not called 'parent education'.

The aim of most parenting programs is to encourage good relationships between parents and each of their children. Underlying these parenting programs is the importance of children's psychological wellbeing. These days emotional intelligence is seen as an important consideration for both parents and children (and it is also important for grandparents). Emotional intelligence means awareness of our own feelings and emotions, managing our own moods in ways that are appropriate to particular situations, self-motivation, and empathy so that the feelings of others are recognised through both verbal and non-verbal cues. Emotional intelligence is the basis for relationships, conflict resolution and for negotiations and it is important for parents to recognise in themselves and to develop in their children. Emotional health is important to effective learning; increasing emotional intelligence can continue throughout life.

Parenting programs are usually aimed at parents of children in particular age groups—babies and toddlers, preschool children, middle childhood (primary school) and adolescents—and usually cover most of the following topics that are important to good parenting:

- An understanding of the differing *development needs of children* as they grow so that parenting supports the gradual maturation of each child. Parents often assume that children are more mature than they actually are.

- *Assertiveness* rather than anger in setting limits for children.

- *Skills in conflict resolution* and problem solving.

- *Empathic listening* so that parents allow their children to speak and express their feelings, thus improving communication and support, and as part of the growth of emotional intelligence.

- Recognition that adolescents need *increased independence*, while acknowledging that they also need limits.

Although there are many theoretical approaches underpinning parent education programs it is recognised that there is not just one way of being an effective parent. Parents have different values systems, personalities, interests, family backgrounds, levels of education and their own social and emotional characteristics, so it is unlikely that any one approach to parenting could be effective with all parents. Although there is no recipe for the ideal parent there are many ways to assist parents to improve their skills.

Parenting education is not always called 'parent education' because some parents are reluctant to undertake such courses. Some parents may feel that they will be seen as inadequate or exposed if they attend classes. As a result, parent education often goes by different names so that parents are not deterred by the name. 'Parent education' programs may focus on children and their needs rather than on the parents. Playgroups provide parents with peer support and information about parenting and children's development, while providing opportunities for children to play together.

The parents in these groups learn through seeing appropriate parenting behaviour modelled, and through information provided both directly and indirectly about their children's needs and development. New mothers' groups work similarly by providing peer support and information during the early stages of children's lives.

Many parents want information about parenting and seek books, magazines and videos as well as more formal forms of parenting education. There are many pre-packaged parenting courses which are available and are often offered by agencies such as schools, preschools and community organisations. However, some courses suit some parents better than others, and 'one size does not fit all'. Some programs focus more on children's behaviour and forms of regulation, some on parent behaviour and responses, and some focus on parent–child interaction. But as noted earlier, not all parents want to attend parenting courses, especially if it means regular attendance over a number of weeks.

Parenting is a commitment for life, and information in some form, often informal, is needed over the life-cycle, as successful parenting requires changes in response to children's changing needs. Transition points in the lives of children and their families are times when parents often actively seek information about their children's changing needs and are open to suggestion. Transitions are also usually accompanied by some stress until family members adjust to the new situation and the new set of expectations, and so they are often looking for information and assistance. The major transitions in family life are pregnancy, the birth of a child, a child starting primary school, starting secondary school, leaving school and finding work or starting tertiary education. Developmentally the transitions are less clear but usually focus on the infant and toddler, the preschool child, middle childhood (or primary school years), adolescence, youth and adulthood.

The following briefly lists the major transitions in children's lives as they affect both the children and their parents. These transitions are a mixture of the externally imposed transitions that exist in our society and the biological and developmental stages of childhood. They also relate to some of the information on child development in the previous section. Because of their own experience as parents, grandparents are usually aware of these transitions and can look back on their own experience as parents. But grandparents must also recognise that things have changed significantly since that time. As my four grandchildren proceed through the various transitions in their young lives I become aware each time of just how out-of-date I have become on what is happening in the various preschool and school settings. It is useful for grandparents to remind themselves of these transitions as they are also likely to affect their own relationships with their grandchildren. Perhaps even more importantly, grandparents will then have a better idea of what the parents are dealing with, and are more likely to be supportive and understanding of their roles.

Pregnancy

Even before birth, babies are part of a social world and can hear their mother's voice and those of the people around them. At birth they are ready for social contact and will communicate with their parents through facial expressions. Research on infants shows us:

> The mother's level of stress, her diet, whether or not she smokes, her cycles of activity, all become part of the unborn baby's experience. Babies are individuals from birth and there are strong differences in the way they behave which is often ignored in advice to parents. By about the 36th week of pregnancy babies have started to develop their own restful and active phases; they will also be noticing more about what is going on around them and will respond to stimulus such as sound (Murray & Andrews 2001, p. 17).

Birth to two years

The issues with children in this age group revolve around feeding, sleep, developmental matters, attachment problems, and adjusting to child care of some sort if the parents are both employed. The big concern when the baby first comes home from hospital is the adjustment of the parents to having a new baby, particularly if it is their first child. The birth of the first child is a fundamental transition for the individual as well as for the couple, whether younger or older, and requires adjustment emotionally, physically, socially and financially. The mother in particular faces changes to her identity as she adapts to motherhood. Mothers often expect too much of themselves, and after the birth find that the baby takes up more time than they had expected, that they are extremely tired, and that they have relationship adjustments to make. Almost one in ten women experience some degree of postnatal depression. Mothers sometimes cannot achieve their own expectations and may be overwhelmed by images of the 'perfect mother'. Grandparents can make a significant contribution to their grandchild at this time, depending on their relationship with the mother, by providing respite for the mother by caring for the child and giving her a break, and just by understanding her feelings.

Early childhood—2–5 years

The concerns regarding children at this age are often developmental and include behaviour management, social development, eating and nutrition, and sometimes adjusting to child care and later preschool.

Parents, but particularly mothers, face a range of concerns in their children's preschool years. Many mothers return to paid work and must decide how to care for their children, although for most this is part-time work only. Many grandparents are able to assist by providing child care at this stage. For mothers, and for some fathers, this is a most concerning transition and as their child adjusts to alternative care mothers are likely to feel guilty, and often feel tired and overworked as well.

The second transition, but one which is usually less stressful for parents, is when children start attending preschool. Because many child care centres also have preschool programs available, this is not such a difficulty for children who attend child care. Preschool is usually seen as being beneficial for the child in an educational sense, and an important preparation for starting school. Most children adjust to preschool—often for only half a day several days a week—with few problems. Preschool also provides somewhere parents can learn more about children's development and parenting.

Middle childhood—6–12 years

A major transition for young children and for their parents is when children start primary school. It is a time when children start moving away from their parents, and the teacher becomes an important person in their lives. School is something which most young children look forward to although they may also have some fears. Preschools often prepare the children for this transition by arranging for the children to visit their primary school, meet the teachers and see their classrooms towards the end of the last year of preschool. But for some children the reality is often more difficult than they expected. They get tired because the days are longer, although many schools reduce the hours at the start of the year. Teachers in primary schools have a different training background from preschool teachers, and have different expectations of the children. The classroom is much more formal than early childhood settings where children have lots of choice in their activities. Some children may find it difficult to have to follow the teacher's instructions and to do what everyone else is doing, until they adjust.

Children in this age group are developing socially, emotionally, physically and intellectually and becoming increasingly independent. They are also developing their own particular interests and becoming aware of their own skills and weaknesses. Parents may be concerned about the educational progress of their child, their children's friendships—and sometimes their lack of friends—their behaviour, and sometimes bullying by other children.

Adolescence—12–18 years

At this age level, and before, children need information about the changes in their bodies and their emotions that take place during these years. Starting secondary school is a major transition for both children and parents. Children go from being the 'biggest fish' in the primary school pond to the 'tiniest tiddler' in the secondary school. In primary school they were the biggest and most dominant children, but when they start secondary school they are the youngest and smallest, amongst large numbers of sometimes frightening older children. They also go from having one classroom teacher who knows them very well to being taught by many teachers who may not even know them by name. Children are sometimes overwhelmed by this transition. Children who have particular problems or learning difficulties can fall by the wayside at this point and it can be the start of a downward spiral if there is no intervention to support them. Parents frequently do not know how to help their children at this stage and find the parent–child relationship difficult. Grandparents who have a good relationship with a grandchild of this age may find that grandchildren tell them more than they tell their parents. On the other hand, they may find that their grandchild no longer wants to spend time with them at all.

The stress that children feel on starting secondary school is often also felt by parents who want to assist their children, but may not know how to, or who to approach. Parents require support and information at this stage and it is an ideal time for supportive intervention particularly from the school. Most schools these days have student support teachers and year level coordinators who are there to assist not only the teachers and children but also the parents.

As secondary school children grow and develop they become increasingly concerned with establishing themselves independently from their parents. Peer groups become more important, and isolated adolescents may become withdrawn and can become depressed. Sexuality and relationships become a matter of great concern for adolescents. Parents are often concerned about the extent to which they can impose limits on their teenager's behaviour, how much freedom to allow, and they fear drug use and sexual activity.

Support for both parents and children needs to be culturally sensitive and appropriate to the needs of this age group, as well as to the needs of families. We know that children in this age group do better if they have connections in the community, whether it is a sporting club, a church or other organisation, because it gives them a sense of connection and belonging.

Youth

When adolescence ends and youth commences is an arguable point. Young people generally do not have full independence these days because of the need for continuing education and the difficulties of obtaining employment. As the end of secondary school approaches, young people and their parents may become anxious about their future, about going on to higher education, about employment, and the fear of unemployment. In their personal lives young people may have concerns about sexuality, identity, independence and financial matters. Youths need support and connections but it is difficult for parents and grandparents to know how to advise them at this stage unless firm foundations are laid earlier in their lives. Parents need good information on current opportunities for their children and advice on what those opportunities will mean for the future, but at this stage young people are largely making their own decisions. Grandparents may be in a better position than anxious parents to take a philosophical and supportive attitude with their grandchildren.

Conclusions for grandparents

This chapter has provided information on what is important in children's development and some of the ways in which parents' education tries to improve the way in which parents bring up their children—your grandchildren. Grandparents can have an important role in the lives of their grandchildren from their birth, but it should complement the way in which they are being brought up. Understanding contemporary approaches to parenting and child development means that grandparents are more likely to feel comfortable about their own relationships with their grandchildren and to better understand the situation of parents.

Grandparents can be additional attachment figures for their grandchildren and provide valuable emotional backup that children need in addition to the relationship with their parents. They can provide support in many ways that assist the grandchildren's family situation by providing child care, baby sitting, and perhaps financial support if this is necessary or possible. It all depends on what is needed, on what the capacity of the grandparents is to provide it, and the extent to which they want to assist and how much they are allowed to assist. When grandchildren are troubled, grandparents may be mentors and mediators as they try to sort things out. Grandparents can open up the world to grandchildren in ways that are different from parents. Because relationships are so important to children, it does not matter what the focus of any activity is, it will have an emotional benefit as well as be an enjoyable activity in its own right.

References

Bronfenbrenner, U 1986, 'Ecology of family as a context for human development: research perspectives', *Developmental Psychology*, vol. 22, no. 6, pp. 723–42.

Goleman, D 1996, *Emotional intelligence: why it can matter more than IQ?*, Bloomsbury, London.

Leach, P 1986, *Your growing child: from babyhood through adolescence*, Alfred A. Knopf, New York.

Leach, P 1996, *Spanking a shortcut to nowhere*, Project NoSpank, viewed 9 March 2006, (www.nospank.net/leach.htm).

Leach, P 1997, *Your baby and child: from birth to age five*, Alfred A. Knopf, New York.

Leach, P (n.d.), *Discipline and cooperation*, Baby Centre, viewed 9 March 2006, (http://www.babycentre.co.uk/refcap/539845.html).

Linke, P 1996, 'Resilience', *Forum on Child and Youth Health*, vol. 4, no. 2, pp. 3–8.

McCain, M & Mustard, F 1999, *Early years study: final report*, Ontario Children's Secretariat, Toronto.

McGregor, H, ACT Community Advocate 2004, Farewell address, Canberra.

Maley, B 2001, 'Corporal punishment is not all bad', 15 February, ON LINE opinion, viewed 9 March 2006, (http://www.onlineopinion.com.au/view.asp?article=1975).

Murray, L & Andrews, L 2000, *Your social baby: understanding babies' communication from birth*, ACER Press, Melbourne.

National Crime Prevention 1999, *Pathways to prevention: developmental and early intervention approaches to crime in Australia*, Attorney General's Department, Canberra.

National Scientific Council on the Developing Child 2004, *Young children develop in an environment of relationships*, Working Paper No. 1, viewed 6 April 2006, (www.developingchild.net/reports.shtml).

National Scientific Council on the Developing Child 2005, *Excessive stress disrupts the architecture of the developing brain*, Working Paper No. 3, viewed 6 April 2006, (www.developingchild.net/reports.shtml).

Newby, J & Andrew, L 2005, *Teen Brain*, Catalyst, 28 July, ABC Television, viewed 10 April 2006, (www.abc.net.au/catalyst/stories/s1424747.htm).

Oakley, A 1992, *Social support and motherhood*, Blackwell, Oxford.

Ochiltree, G 1999, *The first three years*, Brotherhood of St Laurence, Fitzroy, Vic.

Ochiltree, G & Edgar, D 1981, *The changing face of childhood*, Discussion Paper No.4, Australian Institute of Family Studies, Melbourne.

Plomin, R & Loehlin, J 1985, 'Genetic and environmental components of "environmental" influences', *Developmental Psychology*, vol. 21, no. 3, pp. 391–402.

Ramsburg, D 1997, *The debate over spanking*, ERIC Digest, ERIC Clearinghouse on Elementary and Early Childhood Education, Urbana IL, viewed 9 March 2006, (http://www.ericdigests.org/1997-4/spanking.htm).

Rutter, M 1990, 'Psychosocial resilience and protective mechanisms', in J Rolf, A Masten, D Cicchetti, K Neuchterlein & S Weintraub (eds), *Risk and protective factors in the development of psychopathology*, Cambridge University Press, New York.

Shonkoff, J & Phillips, D 2000, *From neurons to neighbourhoods: the science of early childhood development*, National Academy Press, Washington.

Shore, R 1997, *Rethinking the brain: new insights into early development*, Families and Work Institute, New York.

Taylor, N 2005, 'Physical punishment of children: international legal developments', *NZ Family Law Journal*, vol. 5, no. 1, pp. 14–22.

Tomison, A 1996, 'Intergenerational transmission of maltreatment', *Issues in Child Abuse Prevention*, National Child Protection Clearing House Issues Paper, no. 6.

United Nations Children's Fund 1990, *First call for children*, UNICEF, New York.

Reflections

Over the period of time that I have taken to write this book I have learnt much more about grandparents than I had expected. I have learned that being a grandparent is a much more precarious role in the family than I had previously thought. Grandparents are not at the controls of families although they may nominally be at the head. Some may be loved but not respected. Yet it seems to me that grandparents are the glue that holds many families together when the going gets rough and there is nowhere else to turn. Grandparents—but more often the grandmothers—are 'kinkeepers' who hold the family together in good times as well as difficult times by keeping up the family contacts and making opportunities for communication.

The chapters in this book focus mainly around particular issues such as divorce and remarriage, child care and parenting grandchildren, but grandparents' lives are not divided neatly in this way. Many grandparents, including some of those I interviewed, experienced more than one of these issues in their family. Some grandparents were quite reflective about their situation; some kept their difficulties to themselves; and others just got on with their lives and accepted their lot. Sometimes guilt and shame play a part, particularly when they have mixed feelings about the life situations of their children and grandchildren.

Families without grandparents available are in many ways disadvantaged. Grandparents provide child care in many forms, not simply long day care for infants and toddlers and picking up grandchildren from school and preschool, but stepping in when parents are ill, or when they have been let down with other arrangements. An increasing number of grandparents have taken over the parenting of grandchildren when the parents cannot do so. These grandparents are the unsung heroes in our society and not only save their grandchildren from the often poor outcomes of foster care but make a contribution to society and the future of these children in ways which cannot be given monetary value.

Often grandparents experience a strain between their expectations of the grandparent role and the reality that evolves over time. Grandparents usually begin so optimistically when their first grandchild is born, and at that time most do not suspect that their role may be a rocky one. Grandparents with more than one set of grandchildren may play very different roles with the different families, some of which are more satisfying than others. While many grandparents enjoy their time with grandchildren, others have a much more difficult task. It is not always easy being a grandparent and trying not to interfere or criticise, even when you feel it may be justified.

I sometimes feel quite angry that as a society we do not fully recognise how much many of our grandparents are contributing to the coming generations. I feel especially angry when I hear politicians talking about the ageing population and how much they are costing society; this gives no consideration to how much many older people are giving back to society. It is not simply money that grandparents give to their children and grandchildren—although many do that too—but attention, interest, love and time. They are contributing to the coming generations in ways that are not easy to measure.

Like everything else in life, grandparenting does not stay the same and it has its ups and downs. Grandchildren grow older and so do we. Family circumstances change; families move closer or further away. More grandchildren are born and others grow up and become independent. Grandparents cannot change the world for their grandchildren, but they can make a difference in their lives provided they are able to stay in touch and are not prevented by circumstances beyond their control.

I wish all grandparents and grandchildren well and hope that the future brings many satisfactions and happiness, although I know that the way will not always be easy. I also hope that the time will come when the role that grandparents play is more fully recognised and that especially those who are bringing up grandchildren receive more support to help them in this important and sometimes overwhelming task.